SIDEWALKS

Sidewalks

Valeria Luiselli

Translated from the Spanish by
Christina MacSweeney

COFFEE HOUSE PRESS

MINNEAPOLIS

2014

First published in the United States by Coffee House Press, 2014

COPYRIGHT © Valeria Luiselli, 2010

ENGLISH TRANSLATION © Christina MacSweeney, 2013

First published in Spanish as *Papeles falsos* by Sexto Piso, Mexico, 2010

First published in English by Granta Books, Great Britain, 2013

INTRODUCTION © Cees Nooteboom, 2013

ENGLISH TRANSLATION OF INTRODUCTION © Laura Watkinson, 2013

COVER DESIGN by Nathan Burton Design Ltd., nathanburtondesign.com

COVER PHOTOGRAPHS Street scene © Derek Shapton at Gallery Stock,
Post-it note © iStockphoto

"Passionément" from *Le chant de la carpe* by Ghérasim Luca, copyright © 1986.
Reprinted by permission of José Corti, Paris.

Coffee House Press books are available to the trade through our primary
distributor, Consortium Book Sales & Distribution, cbsd.com or
(800) 283-3572. For personal orders, catalogs, or other information, write to:
info@coffeehousepress.org.

Coffee House Press is a nonprofit literary publishing house. Support from
private foundations, corporate giving programs, government programs, and
generous individuals helps make the publication of our books possible.
We gratefully acknowledge their support in detail in the back of this book.

Library of Congress Cataloging-in-Publication Data

Luiselli, Valeria, 1983–
[Essays. Selections. English]
Sidewalks / Valeria Luiselli ;
translated from the Spanish by Christina MacSweeney.
pages cm
ISBN 978-1-56689-356-5 (pbk.) ISBN 978-1-56689-357-2 (e-book)
I. MacSweeney, Christina, translator.
II. Luiselli, Valeria, 1983– Papeles falsos. English.
III. Title.
PQ7298.422.U37P3613 2014
864'.7—DC23
2013035162

To Álvaro
To Maia

Contents

Introduction

Sometimes unexpected things happen that fit together so perfectly it seems as though the ultimate computer that controls and watches over everything does exist after all. A couple of years ago, when I was in Bogotá, I received an e-mail from Karaat, a Dutch publishing house I did not know, asking me to write a foreword for a book by a young Mexican writer I had never heard of. I asked my Colombian host, the poet Pedro Alejo Gómez, who was once the Colombian ambassador to the Netherlands and now runs the Poetry House in Bogotá, if he knew her, but no, he had never heard of her either. Now, it is not the case that books by authors and poets from one Latin American country are sold or discussed in all the other countries on that continent—far from it. Which is why it came as a double surprise when that same day, in a large bookstore in Bogotá, I spotted her book: a slim, crimson edition without any adornment, just the laconic title, *Papeles falsos,* and her name, Valeria Luiselli.

In the days that followed, I traveled around Colombia, to Popayán and Leticia and Cartagena de Indias, with the book in my luggage, and right from the start I realized that I had treated myself to a surprise present.

There is no place better for reading than a hotel room. In tropical Leticia, on the Amazon, the light was yellowish and the room a cavernous yet stifling brick chamber with a groaning ceiling fan, but with the book I was on familiar ground, in the cemetery of Venice, beside the grave of Joseph Brodsky, which I had visited myself years ago for my book *Tumbas*. And perhaps that is the explanation: when you have written about something yourself, you are better able to absorb what another person writes about the same subject. But even though I had felt tremendous respect for Brodsky since once hearing him read at Poetry International in Rotterdam, Luiselli's Brodsky was different from mine; she clearly enjoyed a far deeper affinity with him. At the cemetery of San Michele, I had gone in search of the dead, but she was looking for Brodsky. It was for him that she had gone to Venice—and that is a different kind of journey.

Luiselli may have been young (when she wrote these essays she was in her early twenties), but here was someone who could write in an extremely personal way about her quest to find an admired author, and about her stay in the city that Brodsky himself had written about so magnificently. But, once again, *her* Venice is a different city from his. She arrives feeling ill, finds a room in a convent, gets locked out, and contemplates sleeping on a bench. A friend helps her out and she is soon registered as a resident of the comune of Venice, with local health insurance. This may seem no more than a curious detail, but there is more to it than that. Random things happen to some people; openness is sometimes rewarded with what Luiselli herself refers to as papeles falsos, false papers, particularly when it is the kind of openness with which she views and describes the world. When you under-take a journey with Luiselli, whether in Mexico, flying above the ocean, or in New York, you are traveling with a way of seeing and thinking that belongs to another person; it is sui generis, and you are made to think in a way that is not automatically your own. You find yourself musing about the "excess of identity" that a face takes on over the course of time, about the disappointment of long-awaited first encounters with the dead and the living, about what words *really* are and if their meanings can win out over their letters, and about the motionlessness of maps and the tautological horror of those screens on transatlantic flights, where you can watch the icon of the plane you are sitting inside moving, one millimeter at a time, over the blue emptiness of an image of the ocean.

The tone of her writing is that of the flâneur and the philosopher, as the rhythm of her walking (and cycling—there is an entire passage about being a flâneur on a bicycle, and that in Mexico City of all places!) accompanies her thoughts about architecture and what it does to people, and about empty spaces in the city; this is thinking with a background of asphalt and sidewalk.

The influence of Europeans such as Benjamin, Kracauer, and Baudelaire is never denied, and yet all of her vivid musings retain a Mexican accent, and her openness results in the most remarkable encounters: elderly ladies, security guards, doormen, a Chinese neighbor sitting at his computer, whom she only ever looks at through her window, never exchanging a word with him. This is an idiosyncratic and solitary world that never loses its connection with the world outside.

For the urban nomad, outside has become inside, and vice versa.

What is actually going on in this book? What makes it so enchanting? Because it is, even though that word does not entirely seem to fit with what is at times a high degree of abstraction, with pertinent statements that make the reader pause after a few words and briefly tread water before rereading: "To locate the grave, the definitive inscription we're looking for, it's necessary to examine the veining of the marble closely."

It must be the combination of candor and intelligence, each of which, in its own way, results in a particular method of looking and writing. You need to be good at looking in order to know where you are not, because only then do you know where you actually are. You must coolly convey your discovery of the absurd detail and master the art of hilarious understatement. You also have to be able to hear that the name "Mexican Commission on Limits" will turn your story about the Mexican Map Library—which is intriguing enough in itself even without the addition of the Commission—into a strange adventure for the reader. And then you have to write about it in such a way that the reader also sees everything: both the long, narrow corridors where "maps hang like perennially damp sheets" and the photograph of the eight members of the Commission, who resemble "the eight doctors in Rembrandt's *The Anatomy Lesson of Dr. Nicolaes Tulp.*" And this must be done with a simple flick of the wrist, suddenly transporting the painter from Leiden and Amsterdam into a Mexican map room with a maneuver that shows us, the readers, precisely what the writer means.

There is no lack of apt references in this book: Wallace Stevens and Nietzsche, Chesterton and Rousseau . . . but none of these names weighs too heavily; they flow between the sentences with their own colors, fragments of a worldview that is fueled by knowledge and an erudition worn lightly, not only by the aimless wanderer who writes here, but also by the readers who allow this natural, fluid intellect to take them by the hand and lead them to unexpected places.

I have visited Mexico City often enough, but I have never seen its immensity with these eyes: "a wave of mercury that never quite breaks against the mountain range; the streets and avenues are pet-rified folds in an overflowing, ghostly lake." This is her view upon landing "on that great desert lake." Yet the tears Luiselli sheds at that moment stem not from the sight of that city far below, but from a simple resistance to the "descent to a future world," which evokes fear and a form of sadness, and to a world laid out on a grid pattern to which she will once again have to submit. Mexico City or New York, the city as an ocean of sidewalks and buildings, as a form of puzzle on a map—the writing of the contemplative loner in the urban behemoth is never entirely free from melancholy.

Essays have no plot, travel books (Chatwin, Theroux) sometimes do, and then there is also the travel book as a collection of essays, and the essay that involves traveling and looking. If my eccentric system of classification applies, then *Sidewalks* belongs to the last of these categories. Evidently Rousseau's *Reveries of a Solitary Walker* served as an inspiration for Luiselli, because even though nature has now turned to stone, a romantic element still remains in this city of millions: the moment of the creative void, of the "relin-gos," which she defines in the same breath as "absences in the heart of the city" and "everything we haven't read." That should be easy enough to resolve. But the twist is a different one: if there is no writing, there can be no reading. So this is about writing as the creation of emptiness: "A writer is a person who distributes silences and empty spaces."

"But perhaps," Luiselli writes near the beginning of her book, "a person only has two real residences: the childhood home and the grave. All the other spaces we inhabit are a mere gray spec-trum of that first dwelling, a blurred succession of walls that finally resolve themselves into the crypt or the urn—the tiniest of the infinite divisions of space into which a human body can fit."

The reader that I am is inclined to disagree with her. There is a third residence for the homeless, and that is in writing; even if in Luiselli's definition that means "drilling walls, breaking windows, blowing up buildings. Deep excavations to find—to find what? To find nothing." Drilling, breaking, blowing up—I have no objections. As long as that "nothing" takes the form it has been given in this book, this paradox is easy for a reader to live with. Because whatever she thinks about it herself ("Nothing was further from the truth, in my life at least, than the metaphor of literature as a habitable place or permanent dwelling"), the relingo that Valeria Luiselli has created with *Sidewalks* is a sanctuary for her readers. Just as there are desert travelers, there must also be readers who feel at home in the seemingly uninhabitable spaces Luiselli depicts so well.

Cees Nooteboom
San Luis

JOSEPH BRODSKY'S ROOM AND A HALF

*There is nothing more productive or more entertaining
than allowing oneself to be distracted
from one thing by another.*

Unknown genius,
possibly a reader of Blaise Pascal

Joseph Brodsky (1940–1996)

Searching for a grave is, to some extent, like arranging to meet a stranger in a café, the lobby of a hotel, or a public square, in that both activities engender the same way of being there and looking: at a given distance, every person could be the one waiting for us; every grave, the one we are searching for. Finding either involves circulating among people or tombs; approaching and scrutinizing their respective features.

To locate the grave, the definitive inscription we're looking for, it's necessary to examine the veining of the marble closely; for the face of the stranger, we must compare our expectations of the imagined profile with the various noses, chins, and foreheads present. We have to read the eyes of strangers, as an epitaph is read, until we find the exact insignia—the lapidary yes-it's-me of the person, alive or dead, waiting for us.

Marcelino Giancarlo (1900–1972)

San Michele is a rectangular island, separated from Venice by a stretch of water and a high wall that encloses its cemetery. From an airplane, the cemetery might resemble an enormous hardcover book: one of those stout, heavy dictionaries in which words—like decomposing skeletons—rest eternally.

There's something ironic about the fact that the poet Joseph

Brodsky is buried there, facing the city in which he was always to be found, though forever just passing through. Perhaps he would have preferred a sepulcher far from Venice. When you come down to it, the city was, for him, a "plan B" or, to use a more literary metaphor, an Ithaca whose attraction consisted of being an always distant, imagined place. What's more, Brodsky once stated in an interview that he wanted to be buried in the Massachusetts woods; or perhaps the right thing would have been to return the body to his native St. Petersburg. But I suppose there's no sense in speculating about a person's last wishes. If will and life are two things impossible to separate, so are death and chance.

It's not easy to find Joseph Brodsky's grave there. Unlike many cemeteries in Europe, San Michele isn't a center of necro-intellectual tourism and so there are no guides or detailed maps, much less a list of the coordinates of its famous dead, like those at, for example, the entrances of Montparnasse and Père Lachaise. Other well-known people—Ezra Pound, Luchino Visconti, Igor Stravinsky, Sergei Diaghilev—are to be found in San Michele, but the location of their graves is only marked by a scarcely visible sign opposite the small, separate section where their remains lie. If you don't know that the notable foreigners are separated from the ordinary Venetians, you can spend hours wandering around between the Antoninos, Marcelinos, and Francescos, without realizing that you'll never find echoes of *The Cantos* or reverberations of *The Rite of Spring*.

Having searched for Brodsky's grave for several hours that afternoon, without even finding Stravinsky's, I was on the point of throwing in the towel. While gathering the strength to make my way to the exit of the cemetery, I sat down in the shade of a tree and smoked a cigarette.

Enea Gandolfini (1883–1917)

In his essay "On Running After One's Hat," G. K. Chesterton writes that if a person were to come across a cow during a country walk, only a true artist would be able to paint it, whereas he, not knowing how to draw the hind legs of quadrupeds, would prefer to paint the soul of that cow. I, who am neither an artist nor Chesterton, wouldn't know how to do either of these things. I've never been among that class of people—whom I greatly envy— capable of losing themselves in the pensive contemplation of a bird in flight, the industrious coming and going of ants, the serene suspension of a spider hanging in its own secretions. I am, unfor- tunately, too impatient to find poetry in nature's gentle rhythms.

But there's no need for a special sensibility toward the animal and vegetable kingdoms in a cemetery. It's enough to sit beneath the cypresses, gnomons of gigantic sundials, to allow oneself be possessed by the life force flourishing among the graves. Maybe it's just the silence that magnifies the frenetic flapping of the insects; just the calm that quickens the languid creeping of the lizards; just the death that animates the dying leaves of the black poplars.

I was about to stub out my cigarette and head for the cemetery gates when there was a sudden outburst of squawks. First just a few, then dozens, and then hundreds—as if squawking were as contagious among birds as laughter among people. The philoso- pher Henri Bergson maintained that laughter can only occur if its object is or resembles the strictly human; that a cat or an umbrella can't provoke laughter unless we see in them a human expression, form, or attitude. Could be. It seemed to me that, at least from a distance, the squawking sounded like the wheezing laughter of the elderly or the slightly insane, and for that reason alone I also burst out laughing in the midst of the silence. In any case, if I didn't admit defeat in the task of finding Brodsky's grave, it was simply down to the sudden rush of good spirits provoked by that prattling of hoarse seagulls. If I didn't find the poet, I could at least check if they were indeed squawks and not elderly Venetians laughing their way through death's door. Besides, why shouldn't I run after a grave or some birds if Chesterton, so fat, so dignified, and so intelligent, had been capable of running after a hat?

Lidia Tempesta (1889–1932)

"If there is an infinite aspect to space," writes Joseph Brodsky, "it is not its expansion but its reduction. If only because the reduction of space, oddly enough, is always more coherent. It's better structured and has more names: a cell, a closet, a grave." Brodsky recounts that the established norm for communal housing in the former Soviet Union was nine square meters per person. In the allocation of meters, he and his parents were lucky since, in St. Petersburg, they shared forty square meters: 13.3 apiece: 26.6 for his parents, 13.3 for him: a room and a half for the three of them.

One day in 1972, Joseph Brodsky, then age thirty-two, left his parents' home in 24 Liteiny Prospekt for the last time. He was exiled to the United States and never returned to St. Petersburg, because every attempt to visit his parents had to pass through the hands of a bureaucrat who considered the visit of a Jewish dissenter from the Communist Party unjustified. Brodsky was unable to attend his mother's funeral, or his father's—a "pointless" visit, said the official letter written by the gentleman behind the glass. His parents died about a year apart, sitting in the same old chair, in front of the only television in that apartment in which the three had lived.

Between that room and a half in St. Petersburg and his tomb in Venice, Brodsky occupied many other temporary spaces: other people's bedrooms, hotel rooms, apartments, prison cells, wards of mental hospitals. But perhaps a person only has two real residences: the childhood home and the grave. All the other spaces we inhabit are a mere gray spectrum of that first dwelling, a blurred succession of walls that finally resolve themselves into the crypt or the urn—the tiniest of the infinite divisions of space into which a human body can fit.

Igor Stravinsky (1882–1971)

The graves of the famous foreigners in the cemetery are not only in a separate section from those of the ordinary Venetians—heaven forbid that a gondolier should lie next to Stravinsky's wife—but there are also divisions among the foreigners. The Russian intellectuals who used to haunt Venice are on one side; everyone else on the other. The strange and ironic thing is that Joseph Brodsky is not to be found among either the Moscow or the Leningrad intelligentsia, but in a different section, next to his great enemy, Ezra Pound. And, in contrast to the others, Brodsky's grave isn't indicated by an official sign at the entrance to the section: instead, some benevolent soul has written his name in correction fluid between that of the writer of *The Cantos* and the arrow showing the direction of the two tombs:

Protestant Section: Ezra Pound (+ Iosif Brodsky) →

I imagined that I'd find at least a handful of groupies eager to leave an amulet or a kiss on Brodsky's grave. But there was no one in the

Protestant section. No one except an elderly woman, laden with every imaginable type of shopping bag filled with her belongings, standing by Ezra Pound's grave. I walked directly toward Brodsky without even nodding, as if marking out my territory: you with Pound, me with Brodsky.

Giuseppina Gavagnin (1824–1911)

On Brodsky's grave, inscribed with the dates 1940–1996 and his name in Cyrillic letters, were chocolates, pens, and flowers. But mostly chocolates. There was not, as is so often the case with graves in Italian cemeteries, a portrait of the deceased set into the stone.

In *Watermark,* his book on Venice, Brodsky writes: "Inanimate by nature, hotel room mirrors are even further dulled by having seen so many. What they return to you is not your identity but your anonymity." In a loosely paradoxical way, anonymity is a characteristic of absence: it is the absence of characteristics. A new-born face is almost devoid of singular expressions, and it gradually gains the features that identify it. But as that countenance ages and acquires greater definition, it simultaneously exposes itself to more and more looks from strangers—or, to follow Brodsky's image, to more hotel room mirrors, in which so many reflections have appeared that they all throw back the same visage, rumpled, like an unmade bed—so it also gradually loses the definition it has gained over the years, as if, being seen so often through strange eyes, it tends to return to its unformed original. This is a good thing, because the excess of definition that a face acquires with time, and which would perhaps otherwise culminate in a monstrous excess of identity—in a pained grimace, an unfriendly scowl, a worried frown—is balanced by the simultaneous loss of identity.

In the very beginning and the final stretch, while a person is alive, a face moves asymptotically toward anonymity. It is natural, then, that a dead person should no longer have any face at all. The countenance of the dead must be, in any case, like those white, anonymous petals scattered on a bough to which Pound compares strangers' faces in his poem "In the Station of the Metro."

There was no portrait on Brodsky's gravestone. It seemed appropriate that that definitive stamp of identity was not there; the smooth, opaque gray of the stone was more honest—a reflection of the anonymity of a hotelmensch par excellence, a man of many hotel rooms, many mirrors, many faces. Better to stand by the grave and try to remember some photo of him sitting on a bench in Brooklyn, or bring to mind one of those recordings of his voice, at once powerful but broken, like that of someone who has passed many hours in solitude and acquired conviction through constant doubt.

Luchino Visconti (1906–1976)

The outcome of a long-awaited first meeting is often disappointing. The same is true of an encounter with a dead person, except that there's no need to hide the disappointment: in that sense, a dead person is always more agreeable than a living one. If, on standing before him, we realize that, in fact, we have nothing to do there, that the amusement lay in looking for, rather than finding the grave—what are the stones of Venice going to say to you unless you're Ruskin?—we can move away after a few minutes and the deceased will not reproach us. There's no necessity to be polite to the dead, even though religion has attempted to instill in us absurdly decorous forms of behavior at funeral masses and in cemeteries. Not speaking, praying, and walking slowly with head bowed, hands clasped at waist level, are customs that matter little to those lying six feet under.

That's why the apparently obtrusive presence of the elderly lady standing, as it then seemed to me, deep in thought by Pound's grave turned out to be so timely. She edged toward the shadow of the tree where Brodsky and I were already sharing an uncomfortable silence and began to scratch her legs as if she had fleas. When she'd finished scratching, she moved a little closer and stopped in front of Brodsky's tomb. I stepped aside. With complete calm, like someone carrying out routine domestic chores, she began to steal the chocolates which had been left for the poet. When she'd gathered them all up, she also took the pens and pencils. Looking me straight in the eye, she let out a short, abrupt cackle. Then, as if not wanting to seem impolite, she left a flower on the tombstone—purloined, I suppose, from Pound's grave.

She bent to scratch her legs again, picked up her heavy bags filled with necrological souvenirs, and left the Protestant section. I saw her disappear among the graves, as in that W. H. Auden poem Brodsky was always quoting, "silently and very fast."

FLYING HOME

Churubusco

For an impatient person, there's no torture more cruel than the one that became fashionable on transatlantic flights some time ago, where a map of a portion of the world is projected onto a screen across which a tiny white aircraft advances a millimeter every sixty seconds.

Thirty minutes, an hour, seven hours go by and the icon is still crawling over the same blue surface far from the coasts of the two continents. The best thing would be to sleep or settle down to reading something, only looking back at the screen once another two centimeters of the world map have been conquered. But those of us who lack patience are condemned to fixing our eyes on the tiny aircraft, as if by staring hard enough we could make it advance a little farther.

No invention has been more contrary to the spirit of cartography than these airplane maps. A map is a spatial abstraction; the imposition of a temporal dimension—whether in the form of a chronometer or a miniature plane that advances in a straight line across space—is in contradiction to its very purpose. As surfaces that by nature are immobile and frozen in time, maps don't impose any limitations on the imagination of the person studying them. Only on a static, timeless surface can the mind roam freely.

Hondo

Dust attracts dust. There must be a scientific explanation for this, but I've no idea what it is. All the dust in the Valley of Mexico City accumulates in the Map Library, as if this were its fate, its natural destination. This library has, for several years, and for some unfathomable reason, been housed in the National Meteorological Service building.

One would think that a place that treasures maps, or at least classifies and repairs them, would have a more or less ordered distribution of space. But this is not the case here. It's difficult to navigate your way around the Map Library and—although the space is limited—it's impossible not to lose track of where you are in relation to the entrance or, if there were one, some precise center. If you go into the room where the restoration work used to be undertaken, you no longer know where the corridor with cartographic instruments is; if you're in the small section of maps from the early nineteenth century, you completely lose any sense of the location of the modern North American ones.

In a series of long, narrow corridors, maps hang like perennially damp sheets. To study them you have to put on a surgical mask and gloves. The assistants—students of history or geography, anxious to finish their 480 hours of compulsory community service—help visitors to take the maps down and lay them on one of the large tables near the entrance. Two hands are not enough to carry the sheets—the years weigh down the paper.

The corridors in the Map Library lead to small rooms in which the exhibits are grouped according to geographical region and historical period. The section dealing with the Porfirio Díaz dictatorship (1876–1910) is, naturally, the most organized and best classified

(Positivism did perhaps leave Mexicans some legacy). There, the curator showed me two books of Gulliverian proportions—at least a meter and a half by a meter—tracing the line of the frontier between Mexico and Guatemala in minute detail. My excitement was proportionate to the size of the books when the curator first took them from their heavy chests—mahogany sarcophagi in which they are usually kept, protected from the dust and light.

But, after a brief perusal, the two volumes testifying to the delimitation of the Mexico-Guatemala border turn out to be sadly repetitive: pages and pages of blank paper crossed by a narrow blue strip, now representing the Suchiate River, now the Usumacinta River, with a few incomprehensible annotations that most probably indicate the number of steps taken along the bank in 1882 by one of the members of the Mexican Commission on Limits (never has there been a better name for a commission). This great empty book is, then, the only existing testimony to the line dividing one country from another.

What really grabs the attention are the photos of the members of the Commission on Limits, pasted onto the frontispiece of the first volume. In the individual portraits, they all seem like versions of the dictator Porfirio Díaz, some shorter, others less spruce, but all serious, perhaps conscious of the gravity of their assignment: the definition of the boundaries of a country. Only one photograph gives away what one might imagine to be the true spirit of cartographers. In this image, eight members of the Commission, like the eight doctors in Rembrandt's *The Anatomy Lesson of Dr. Nicolaes Tulp,* are standing around a long table—not so different from those on which pathologists cut up cadavers—scrutinizing a map, and holding cartographic dissection instruments. The photo is an almost exact copy of the Rembrandt painting: the head surgeon, with the authority conferred by the scalpel, poised above the patient; the patient, dead, irremediably passive, at the mercy of the specialist's diagnosis; the apprentices, who are looking in any and every direction except toward the patient, listening—some in stupefaction, others in consternation, and others absentmindedly—to the master's pronouncements. And so too are the cartographers leaning over the map; the country, like the cadaver, awaits a postmortem diagnosis.

In essence, an anatomist and a cartographer do the same thing: trace vaguely arbitrary frontiers on a body whose nature it is to resist determined borders, definitions, and precise limits. How does the doctor know where the tongue finishes and the pharynx really begins? How does the cartographer plot the boundary between one country and another? In the photo, two members of the Commission are lying on the table. One of them is half smiling, complicit in a discovery or an irrevocable judgment: here Mexico—over there Guatemala.

When I asked about the maps showing the original plans of Mexico City, the curator apologized and told me they didn't exist. Legend has it that a Spanish soldier, a certain Alonso García Bravo, traced the design directly onto the ground. There are maps of the city from the sixteenth century, of course, but none precedes the grid plan of the historic center. García Bravo made a few scratches in the damp earth somewhere around 1522 and became the first urban planner of the great capital of New Spain. It's no surprise that it happened that way. Every inhabitant of Mexico City suspects it: if a sketch of the city has ever been made, the pencil scarcely touched the paper, and what is now called "urban planning" is pure nostalgia for the future.

Magdalena

In an airplane, few people are conscious of the physical, absolutely concrete fact of flight. Commercial aircraft—with their minute windows and seats that recline just a few stingy degrees—bear no relationship to the essential nature of what man first glimpsed in the flight of birds. Everyone on board—the fat, the sleepless, the children with short attention spans and bursting eardrums, the hysterical, the Xanax addicts—attempts to ignore the fact, at once beautiful and terrifying, that their bodies are suspended in mid-air. The food is served, the film begins, and the air hostess asks for the plastic blinds to be lowered. Only if we open the blind in an act of rebellion against the dictatorship of the cabin crew, can we see the world there below and, for an instant, comprehend where we are. Viewed from above, that world is immense but attainable, as if it were a map of itself, a lighter and more easily apprehended analogy.

Ameca

In the past, Mexico City was often compared to Venice. The city was once an island crisscrossed by canals and surrounded by great lakes fed by the rivers that flowed down from the steep mountain range enclosing the valley. But it's impossible now to imagine what the conquistador Bernal Díaz del Castillo observed in 1519 when the Spanish army marched along the old Iztapalapa road toward the island of Tenochtitlan, which is today in the center of a waterless city: "[seeing] that paved road, as it ran so straight and flat toward Mexico, we were lost in wonder and said that it was like the enchanted things that are spoken of in Amadis of Gaul, because of the great towers and temples and buildings there in the water, and all made of stone and mortar." No one could now compare the city to something so literary—or so wet.

Magdalena

Some geographical comparisons are more successful than others. I'm willing to concede the analogy between Italy and a boot, between Chile and a chili pepper, and even the one between Manhattan and a crooked phallus. But I don't understand, for example, why people compare the outline of Venice to a fish. If one consults a detailed plan, the city could look like the skeleton of a Paleozoic mollusk. But even that requires a strong imagination. And neither is Boris Pasternak's comparison with a sodden, stony pretzel quite right.

Any analogy involves trickery because it both includes the idea it attempts to explain and, at the same time, moves away from that idea to attain its goal. But certain things—a territory, a map—elude direct observation. Sometimes it's necessary to create an analogy, a slanting light that illuminates the fugitive object, in order to momentarily fix the thing that escapes us. Having studied Venetian maps many times, it's clear to me that, more than anything else, the city is like the pieces of a shattered knee. Venice—the map of Venice—and a knee: taken together, a certain clarity emerges. But what can modern Mexico City be compared to?

Chico de los Remedios

It's a paradoxical fact that Mexico City, which—unlike Berlin, Paris, or New York—does have an exact city center, has not been organized around that central point and so has lost any possible sense of coherence. Or maybe it was the confidence generated by that center that allowed the city to expand indefinitely until it lost its outline, until it overflowed the basin of the Valley of Mexico, which originally contained it.

Perhaps that's why writing about Mexico City is a task doomed to failure. Unaware of this, for a long time I thought that if I were to succeed in this task, I had to follow the traditional route: convert myself, à la Walter Benjamin, into a connoisseuse of benches, a botanist of the urban flora, an amateur archaeologist of the facades in the city center and the spectacular advertising hoardings of the Periférico—the six-lane expressway that once orbited the city but is now merely a deeply embedded inner ring of crawling traffic. With this in mind, I tried walking like a petite Baudelaire through that sickly appendage to the National University known as Copilco: impossible to squeeze out a single line about it. Could Copilco itself be to blame? The writer Fabrizio Mejía says the name comes from the Nahuatl word meaning "place of copies." After repeated strolls through the area, I can assert—without fear of error—that, etymological facts aside, there is nothing to write about that truly ugly part of the city, where the books in university libraries undergo mass reproduction for ten centavos a page. Maybe it really is Copilco's fault.

But neither does the bookish Calle Donceles, in the historical center, suggest anything more than the odd high school memory of first reading Carlos Fuentes's *Aura* or some real-visceral, Bolañoesque ramble.

These lines by Francisco de Quevedo offer an explanation but they give no comfort:

You search for Rome in Rome, oh pilgrim!
And in Rome itself you do not find Rome.

Colmena

Most would accept that our capacity for abstraction exceeds our ability to imagine the concrete world in full detail. The average man is incapable of visualizing the image of an object with an infinite number of details, or one that undergoes constant transformation. But most people find it quite easy to draw a graph or sketch a two-dimensional plan of a house from memory. We need the abstract plane to move around easily, to ravel and unravel possible journeys, plan itineraries, sketch out routes. A map, like a toy, is an analogy of a portion of the world made to the measure of the eye and the hand. It is a fixed superimposition on a world in perpetual motion, made to the scale of the imagination: 1 cm = 1 km.

Piedad

In an essay on the river Spree in Berlin, Fabio Morábito writes: "A river tends to contain the city it crosses and to curb its ambitions, reminding it of its face; without a river, that is, without a face, a city is abandoned to itself and can become, like Mexico City, a blot." Maybe Morábito is right: maybe it all comes down to a problem of hydrodynamics. Mexico City lost its lakes and rivers, one by one. Over time they were drained or piped underground by idiotic, megalomaniac governments who somehow thought it was a good idea to suck the city dry. What were once expanses of water became avenues, car parks, vacant lots, undefined cement-clad stretches.

The earliest maps of Mexico City are the 1524 Nuremberg Map and the Uppsala Plan from 1555 (how they got to Germany and Sweden, respectively, is a mystery). They consist of very few features—main streets, large rectangular areas, a few scattered houses, boats, and fish. It's difficult to tell where is north and where south, but that's not really important; the maps are honest in their way; simple, like haikus. On close inspection, the first maps of the city are nothing more than Cartesian reductions of space, diagrams imposed upon a territory that was, to a great extent, only water.

However, the city of that time did resemble something: "In the center of the salt lake sits the metropolis, like an immense flower of stone," writes Alfonso Reyes in his *Visión de Anahuac*. In the Nuremberg map, the city looks like a perfect, semielliptical cranium submerged in a huge tub. In the Uppsala Plan, it's clearly a human heart preserved in alcohol. It brings to mind some lines by Guillaume Apollinaire:

> *The pensive city, with its weathervanes*
> *On the frozen chaos of the rooftops*
> *Resembles the frozen but varied heart of the poet*
> *With the shrill whirling of so much senselessness.*

There are those who say that Mexico City is like a big pear—a bizarre sister of the Big Apple; the widest part of the fruit to the south and the stalk somewhere around the Basílica de Guadalupe, in the northernmost borough. But on more careful examination, the flesh of the fruit has, in fact, overflowed far beyond its skin.

A contemporary artist—or a child—might represent the pear-city with a silhouette, like the ones drawn in chalk at the scene of a murder, the consequences of which exceed the supposed containment of the outline: pear splattered on tarmac.

The latest map we have of Mexico City (Guía Roji, 2013) doesn't look like anything—anything except perhaps a stain, a trace, a distant memory of something else.

Mixcoac

No comprehensive idea of Mexico City can be formed by walking it. Rousseau's solitary strolls, Walser's or Baudelaire's saunters, the image-walks of Kracauer, and Benjamin's flâneries were all ways of understanding and portraying the new structure of modern cities. But the inhabitants of Mexico City don't have a holistic sense of the place in which they pass their lives because they lack any point of reference. At some stage, the notion of a center, an axis, was lost.

An obvious inference of this would be that Mexico City has to be seen from above in order to be grasped in its totality. I've tried it. But the elevated section of the Periférico offers nothing more than a brief surfacing for air between our everyday clouts of suffocation. Flying over the city at night, one can perhaps, for a few minutes, see it anew. From far above, lights glimmer in the valley and it regains its liquid past: a lake overcrowded with fishing boats. And, on a clear day, from an airplane window, the city is almost comprehensible—a simpler representation of itself, to the scale of the human imagination. But as the airplane descends to earth, one discovers that the grid is floating on what seems to be an indeterminate stretch of gray water. The folds of the valley embody the threat of a wave of mercury that never quite breaks against the mountain range; the streets and avenues are petrified folds in an overflowing, ghostly lake.

Tacubaya

Coming down to land in Mexico City has always given me a sort of reverse vertigo. As the plane approaches the runway and the seats begin to tremble slightly, when the atheists cross themselves and the air hostess makes her final walk along the weightless aisle, I start to feel a force propelling me upward, as if my center of gravity had been displaced, or my body and that runway were identical magnetic poles. Something in me resists the ground.

It's not unusual for some passengers to cry when an airplane takes off—people have come from separations and, on fastening their seat belts, feel one last jolt of detachment. But I imagine that it's not so common to see such a spectacle when the plane finally lands. I've found myself crying on a number of arrivals in Mexico City. As soon as I see the Nabor Carrillo—that impossible, perfectly rectangular little lake near the airport, which from above resembles the San Michele cemetery in Venice, only here the water is surrounded by cement rather than the cement by water—I go to pieces. Nothing noisy, just tears. I have no doubt that this pathetic sight has, on more than one occasion, sparked sincere compassion in the other passengers in my row. (What a shame, they probably think—she must be very unhappy here, poor soul.) But I feel certain that those tears that afflict me on landing have nothing to do with unhappiness. As a child, I put them down to tiredness—tears: a secretion of fatigue. However, with the passage of time, I've concluded they are merely an expression of resistance to the descent to a future world which, as it draws closer, becomes once again immeasurable. Those tears are a simple, moist tribute to landing on that great desert lake fed by rivers that have dried up or been channeled underground, and which today seem like little more than empty, arid words: Churubusco, Hondo, Magdalena, Chico, Ameca, Colmena, Piedad, Mixcoac, Tacubaya.

MANIFESTO À VELO

Stop

Apologists for walking have elevated ambulation to the height of an activity with literary overtones. From the Peripatetic philosophers to the modern flâneurs, the leisurely stroll has been conceived as a poetics of thought, a preamble to writing, a space for consultation with the muses. It is perhaps true that in other times the greatest risk one ran on going out for a walk was, as Rousseau related in one of his *Meditations,* to be knocked down by a dog. But the reality is that, nowadays, the pedestrian can't venture out into the street with the same extravagant spirit and modernist love for the metropolis as the eclectic Swiss writer Robert Walser professed at the beginning of his novel *The Walk:* "One morning, as the desire to walk came over me, I put my hat on my head, left my writing room, or room of phantoms, and ran down the stairs to hurry out into the street."

The urban walker has to march to the rhythm of the city in which he finds himself and demonstrate the same single-minded purpose as other pedestrians. Any modulation of his pace makes him the object of suspicion. The person who walks too slowly could be plotting a crime or—even worse—might be a tourist. Except for those who still take their dogs for a walk, children coming home from school, the very old, or itinerant street vendors, no one in the city has the right to slow, aimless walking. At the other extreme, anyone who runs without wearing the obligatory sports attire could be fleeing justice, or suffering some sort of noteworthy panic attack.

Speed cameras

The cyclist, on the other hand, is sufficiently invisible to achieve what the pedestrian cannot: traveling in solitude and abandoning himself to the sweet flow of his thoughts. The bicycle is halfway between the shoe and the car, and its hybrid nature sets its rider on the margins of all possible surveillance. Its lightness allows the rider to sail past pedestrian eyes and be overlooked by motorized travelers. The cyclist, thus, possesses an extraordinary freedom: he is invisible. The only declared enemy of the cyclist is the dog, an animal obscenely programmed to chase any object that moves faster than itself.

No dogs

If dogs tend to resemble their masters, the similarity is even more pronounced for bicycles and their riders. A bicycle can be found for every temperament: there are melancholy, enterprising, executive, fearsome, nostalgic, practical, nimble, and parsimonious bikes.

Speed limit: 160 km/h

Julio Torri—a self-proclaimed admirer of urban cycling, who wrote a defence of the bicycle in the early 1900s—once pointed out that neither the plane nor the car is proportionate to man since their speed exceeds his needs. The same is not true of the bicycle. The cyclist chooses the speed that best fits the rhythms of his body, which, in turn, depend on nothing more than his own limitations.

The bicycle is not only noble in relation to body rhythms: it is also generous to thought. For anyone with a tendency to digress, the sinuous company of the handlebars is perfect. When ideas are gliding smoothly along in straight lines, the two wheels of the bicycle carry both rider and ideas in tandem. And when some stray thought afflicts the cyclist and blocks the natural flow of his mind, he only has to find a good steep slope and let gravity and the wind work their redemptive alchemy.

Pedestrian crossing

If, in the past, strolling was emblematic of the thinker, and while there may be places where it's still possible to walk about deep in thought, this has little relevance to the inhabitants of most cities nowadays. The urban pedestrian carries the city on his shoulders and is so immersed in the maelstrom that he can't see anything except what is immediately in front of him. Moreover, those who use public transport are restricted to a seat's-worth of privacy and a few meters of visual range. And the motorist, who travels vacuum-packed in his car, unable to hear or smell or see or really exist in the city, is no exception: his soul is blunted at every traffic light, his gaze is the slave of the spectacular hoardings, and the mysterious, anarchic laws of the traffic set the standard for the variations of his mood.

For Salvador Novo, poet and cofounder of the modernist magazine *Los Contemporáneos,* "the step-by-step matching of our internal rhythms—circulation, respiration—to the deliberate universal rhythms that surround, lull, rock, yoke us, is renounced when we set off in an automobile, at an insane speed, to simply cancel out distances, change locations, swallow up miles." The cyclist, in contrast to the person traveling by car, achieves that lulling, unworried speed that frees thought and allows it to go along a piacere. Skimming along on two wheels, the rider finds just the right pace for observing the city and being at once its accomplice and its witness.

Speed bumps

Of course, the bicycle can be used for other ends besides mere carefree travel: there are delivery men, cycle rickshaw drivers, and even bicycle knife grinders, a species now almost extinct. Not to mention that semialien life form: racing cyclists, sheathed to resemble undernourished scuba divers, sticking their tiny tight asses out as they speed through the city. But in spite of these riders who prize the utility of two wheels above its art, riding a bicycle is one of the few street activities that can still be thought of as an end in itself. The person who distinguishes himself from that purposeful crowd by conceiving it as such should be called a cycleur. And that person—who has discovered cycling to be an occupation with no interest in ultimate outcomes—knows he possesses a strange freedom that can only be compared with that of thinking or writing.

Keep your distance

The difference between flying in an airplane, walking, and riding a bicycle is the same as that between looking through a telescope, a microscope, and a movie camera. Each allows for a particular way of seeing. From an airplane, the world is a distant representation of itself. On two legs, we are condemned to a plethora of microscopic detail. But the person suspended over two wheels, a meter above the ground, can see things as if through the lens of a movie camera: he can linger on minutiae and choose to pass over what is unnecessary.

Go

Nowadays, only someone sensible enough to own a bicycle can claim to possess an extravagantly free spirit when he puts on a hat, leaves the writing room, or "room of phantoms," and runs down the stairs to unchain his bicycle and ride out into the street.

ALTERNATIVE ROUTES

Calle Mérida—northbound

Around six in the evening, when that last layer of daylight begins to detach itself from the objects in our living room and the electric light only serves to blur the somewhat unclear outlines of things even further, I feel an urge to leave the apartment. I don't know if it's because matter itself becomes restless with the first shadows of night—as if darkness allows objects to overflow a little beyond themselves and things are on the point of breaking their pact of silence with the world—or if it's just I who can't find peace at that tranquil hour. And it's around that time too that Sara comes back from work and takes out her painting materials. The apartment fills with kettle murmurs, barefoot steps, the pine-forest smell of oils and thinner. I put on the old hat I've taken to wearing, get on my bicycle, and go out into the streets of the Colonia Roma.

A few blocks later, I chain my bike to a lamppost and go into the Librería del Tesoro—one of the few bookstores left in the neighborhood. I look for a Portuguese dictionary, which, once again, I can't find. I shall have to continue putting off my good intentions to learn Portuguese the proper way. Instead, I buy two books of Brazilian poetry and a postcard for forty-seven pesos. I'm beginning to suspect that what I like about Portuguese is misunderstanding it.

Some years ago, I attended a conference in which two experts were discussing the Portuguese term *saudade*. It was one of those events where the speakers establish a hierarchical relationship between themselves and the audience, the members of which come away with the sole idea that they haven't really understood what was being discussed. The first lady—whom I had trouble taking seriously as she vaguely resembled a wrinkled version of the child Shirley Temple—argued that *saudade* is one of those untranslatable words that can only be understood by those who love, experience pleasure, and suffer in Portuguese. If you are not a lusophone, the other speaker declared, you have no right to borrow *saudade*. Could be. But then, why not just steal the word?

It's started raining outside, so I grab a stool and sit down between two sets of shelves to take a look at my new books. I search for any trace of the word *saudade* among their pages. Nothing. But some lines I half understand jump out at me:

> *calçadas que pisei*
> *que me pisaram*
> *como saber no asfalto da memoria*
> *o ponto em que comença a fantasia?*

I'm not sure what the lines say, though the words *ponto, asfalto, memoria,* and *fantasia* form a dim constellation of possible meanings—perhaps all connected to saudade. When we have only a partial knowledge of a language, the imagination fills in the sense of a word, a phrase, or a paragraph—like those drawing books where the pages are covered with dots that, as children, we had to join with a crayon to reveal the complete image. I don't understand Portuguese, or I understand it as partially as any other Spanish speaker. If I say "saudade," it will always be joining the dots of a foreign page.

Turn left at Durango

Saudade isn't homesickness, lack, or longing. The Finnish *kaihomielisyys*—though it contains smooth, mellifluous sounds—expresses only its most desolate sense. The German *Sehnsucht* and the Icelandic *söknudur* seem to suck out the meaning of the word; the Polish *tesknota* sounds bureaucratic; the Czech *stesk* shrinks, cringes, cowers; and the Estonian *igatsus* would come closer if spoken backwards. Maybe saudade isn't saudade.

Circle Plaza Rio de Janeiro—clockwise

Although saudade is loosely related to melancholy and nostalgia, the origins of the word are unclear. It's possible that it was the name of a Portuguese sailing ship, the São Daede, which, in 1497, preceded Vasco da Gama in the exploration of the Indian Ocean. It may be derived from the Latin *solitudinis* or the desert *saudah* of the Arabs. It could also have been a musical instrument from the coast of Mozambique, or just as possibly the name of a voluptuous woman from the jungles of Guinea Bissau.

Left again at Orizaba

Melancholy used to be a humor, an excess of black bile. Aristotle thought it was a divine gift, only given to men of true genius. In the Middle Ages, melancholy's fetid vapors were thought to dim understanding and perturb the soul. Of the four bodily humors—phlegm, yellow bile, blood, and melancholy—the last was the coldest and driest. The melancholic person had sunken eyes and a taciturn expression: he was circumspect, stern, and solitary;

insomniac and given to nightmares; passionate and jealous. He had a waxen complexion, was flatulent, his excretions were painful, his urine colorless and sparse. The cause of melancholy, according to popular wisdom, was poor diet, and it was cured by purges, unguents, poultices, and bloodletting.

With time, the number of causes of melancholy grew and became less worldly:

> The planet Saturn
> Idleness
> Excess of knowledge
> Witches and wizards

The cures, however, remained terrestrial. In 1586, in a letter to an imaginary melancholic patient, Dr. Timothy Right recommended that he avoid:

> Cabbage, dates, olives
> Leguminous plants and chickpeas
> Pig meat, mutton, and goat
> Seals and porpoises

Continue along Orizaba—ride on sidewalk to avoid traffic

Bastard daughter of melancholy, the term *nostalgia* inherited the characteristics of black bile but never achieved its former divine status. The magic humors of mother melancholy evaporated in the three dry syllables of her aseptic daughter: nos-tal-gia. Like other such "algias" as cephalalgia and neuralgia, nostalgia was, in the seventeenth century, firmly fixed as a clinical condition. It's no surprise that its appearance coincides with the era in which "afflictions of the soul" became "pathologies of the psyche."

Nostalgia was the invention of Johannes Hofer, a military doctor. Hofer treated Swiss soldiers who, after long periods in foreign lands, suffered from a set of common symptoms: headaches, sleeplessness, heaviness of heart, hearing voices and seeing ghosts. The exiled soldiers took on a gloomy, almost phantasmagorical aspect—they walked around as if absent from the world and in their imaginations confused the past and the present.

Hofer made note of every one of the soldiers who came into his consulting room during the year 1688, and as the number of nostalgic cases on his list grew, so too did his impatience to organize that series of coincidences into a single pathology. Like someone who awaits the passage of a comet in order to be able to place his name on the celestial map, Hofer waited for the arrival of the very last soldier to christen his hypothesis. Then, satisfied, he closed his casebook and began his *Medical Dissertation on Nostalgia*.

Nostalgia, according to Hofer, is an illness that expresses itself in a specific symptom: pain (*algia*) for the home (*nostos*). And like any other illness, remedies can be found to treat it. If the nostalgia is a longing for something concrete, it may perhaps be weakened by eclipsing the memory of what was with the overwhelming presence of what is. Leeches, for example, may distract the mind from the abstract pain of the loss of home by the very real pain of their bites. Opium constructs inebriating scenarios that mist the memory of the past.

But the soldiers eventually became immune to such palliatives. After many experiments, Hofer concluded that nothing produced better results than sending them back home.

Turn right at Tabasco

There is no such thing as a nostalgic or "saudadic" child, but there are melancholy ones. When I was about five years old someone told me you could dig a tunnel all the way to China. We were living in Central America and I thought I could save my family the expense of the plane fare by digging my way home. If someone had got as far as China, I could surely get to Mexico, which was much closer. I asked my father to tell me the exact direction of our house there and he drew me a map. I started digging a tunnel in a corner of the garden.

The tunnel project dragged on for several weeks, until I began to get bored.

I was on the point of abandoning the hole—by that time quite deep—when I suddenly hit something solid: a possible treasure chest. The three following mornings, I dug around that hard surface and completely forgot the original plan. Then I extended the treasure hunt. In the end, I made holes all over the garden, but never found anything more than a few earthworms and the water tank. Naturally, my parents began to lose patience. They ordered me to call a halt to the excavation. I obeyed, but it seemed to me that I should put the holes to good use by burying something in each of them. In one I hid some marbles, in another a toy train, and in a third a horrible paperweight with a snowscape. In the main hole, where the treasure that turned out to be a water tank had been, I placed the map my father had drawn for me. I thought that some future child—who, coincidentally, would also be Mexican and living in that same house—could reconstruct the story of the holes. Making use of more modern instruments than mine, that child would find the map and come to visit me in Mexico. And if too many years went by and I died, there would at least be a trace of my passage through that garden. From that moment, the garden stopped being an invitation to return to Mexico and became instead the promise of the future discoveries of that other child: I was cured of my precocious melancholic temperament—like a patient in the Middle Ages—by a bit of earth.

Ride on sidewalk for one block

Saudade, which retains some form of pain in the gliding movement between its first vowels, brings to mind those things that are at once beautiful and a little sad: boats, willows, saurian lizards, a bough.

Make a right at Chihuahua

The melancholy temperament was once the emblem of genius; black bile a divine substance. Aristotle was responsible for spreading this rumor, the echo of which was contested in the Middle Ages but apparently heard again by the Romantics and then by the poètes maudits and the aesthetes. But later, melancholy became mere aggravated emotionalism; and it is perhaps Sigmund Freud who bears the greatest responsibility for finishing off its founding myth. Freud democratized melancholy: once the psychiatrist's couch had appeared on the scene, the illustrious and the intellectual were no longer the jealous owners of a divine illness. By the early twentieth century, melancholy had ceased to be the way of life and state of the soul of poets and had become a contemptible trait, only worthy of hysterical females on the couch. The same is true of nostalgia, which in time was no longer a hypochondria of the heart or a mental illness, but something from which maybe only Uruguayans and Norwegians suffer. Melancholy and nostalgia eventually ended up in the same bottomless pit: depression (according to the definition of the International Classification of Diseases).

Right again at Frontera

Sara insists that the most exact Spanish translation of *saudade* is "tiricia." I've searched everywhere for definitions of that term. There are several on the internet:

> Dentera (synonym): a disagreeable sensation in the teeth and gums on eating bitter substances and hearing certain unpleasant noises, corresponding to the English idea that something "sets one's teeth on edge."

> Ictericia (synonym): a disease produced by the buildup of bilious pigment in the blood, the external sign of which is yellowness of the skin and the conjunctiva; in other words, jaundice.

> In El Salvador: laziness, negligence, ill humor.

> Infantile depression.

Two blocks on—make a right at Zacatecas

Now that melancholies and nostalgias are no longer owned by doctors, the "Ulysses Syndrome" has been discovered. In the strap line of a Spanish newspaper that Sara left on the couch some days ago, I read:

> Fifty percent of immigrants develop some form of mental
> disturbance . . . ! A third of illegal immigrants are likely to
> suffer from the "Ulysses Syndrome."

Despite the literary name given to the new pathology, it is also conceived of as a clinical problem. The symptoms of the disease: sadness, crying, stress, headaches, chest pains, insomnia, fatigue, and hallucinations. The remedies: psychiatrists and drugs. In Barcelona there's already a team of doctors treating the affected "undocumenteds." How many pills will be sold before it's discovered that the Ulysses Syndrome can't be cured by medicines? How many years before it is understood that the pain in the chest is nothing more than saudade, a bit of nostalgia, an excess of black bile?

Plaza Luis Cabrera—cross slowly

Commonplaces:

> "Saudade is something you have." You have saudade the way
> you have a plaything. It's a perfect marble, round and never-
> ending. It's a monad in the palm of your hand: a paperweight
> enclosing a miniature snowscape.

> "Saudades are both pleasant and painful." The scabs on knees
> we pick at until we draw blood; the teeth we prod with the
> tip of the tongue until they fall out; the pores on bare skin
> that open on contact with scalding bathwater.

> ⌡ "Saudade is the presence of an absence." A stabbing pain in a
> phantom limb; a crack that opens up suddenly in the asphalt;
> the rivers and lakes of Mexico City; sheets after lovemaking.

> "Saudade is saudade is saudade." A map—of a map.

Turn south onto Orizaba

Wisdom from Cyril Connolly: "Imagination = nostalgia for the past, the absent; it's the liquid solution in which art develops the snapshot of reality."

But the nostalgia isn't always nostalgia for a past. There are things that produce nostalgia in advance—spaces that we know to be lost as soon as we find them—places in which we know ourselves to be happier than we will ever be afterwards. In such situations, the soul twists itself around, as if in a voluntary simulacrum of seeing its present in retrospect. Like an eye watching itself look from the perspective of a later time, it sees that remote present and yearns for it.

Go left at Querétaro—use the sidewalk

Sara is doing an oil painting from a snapshot she took in Madrid some years ago, when we lived there together. It's of a long, narrow street called the Paseo de los Melancólicos, through which we often had to ride home. Along the bank of the river Manzanares— that "liquid irony," as Ortega y Gasset described it, due to its almost total lack of water—the melancholy Paseo de los Melancólicos stretches out like a pleonasm. On one side is a row of gray buildings, each one identical to the last. On the other, a concrete wall behind which one has to imagine that, a few steps away, an attempt at a river flows. In this section of its course, where the waters resemble black bile, the Manzanares has vents—tall tubes sprouting skyward from the water like the chimneys of an old, sunken factory. Nobody knows the purpose of those giant industrial pipes, but on some winter nights they emit a sound like whale song and a fetid vapor that settles on the Paseo de los Melancólicos like a beautiful, suffocating blanket.

Left again at Jalapa

Saudade is a child with a bad squint: he looks ahead with one eye and back with the other. When the right eye urges him to move forward, the left exhorts him to go back. That's why he remains forever motionless in his place and the only steps he's allowed are the ones the soul takes around itself.

Tabasco—make a right—ride against traffic

Sara says that Fernando Pessoa is the personification of saudade. Could be. Over dinner, we read aloud randomly chosen fragments from *The Book of Disquiet,* which has been lying around the house for more than a month—sometimes in her bedroom, sometimes in mine, often in the kitchen, almost always in the bathroom. As she reads, I imagine Pessoa, standing at the window of his small attic, on the fourth floor of a house in Lisbon's Biaxa district, looking down over the haphazard agglomeration of roofs in the tawny evening light. If he were to go down the stairs to the street, he'd perhaps cross to the other sidewalk to buy a packet of fresh tobacco; in the doorway he'd meet Esteves, who would nod in greeting. But, ever ill prepared for spontaneous meetings, Pessoa wouldn't be able to look him in the eye. If, on leaving the establishment, he were then to walk down to Rua dos Douradores and on to La Travessa do Almada, he'd pass the office where his boss, Senhor Moitinho de Almeida, would be waiting for him to arrive at half past eight on the dot the following morning. Stopping off for a short time in the restaurant that now bears his name, he'd see Bernado Soares, with whom he would have a glass of wine and a bowl of kale and chicken soup. Continuing along the street to Rua do São Mamede, he'd go up the steps at São Crispim and, a few meters farther on, reach Rua da Saudade. Maybe there, leaning over a balcony, he'd discover another of his heteronyms: a melancholic South African from Cape Town, a professor of English literature, specialist in the mysteries of the iambic pentameter. But Pessoa doesn't move away from the window—as I don't really move from my spot while I write.

> *I invoke myself and find nothing.*
> *I go to the window and see the street in absolute clarity.*
> *I see the shops, see the sidewalks, see the cars passing by.*
> *I see the live, clothed beings passing each other by.*
> *I see the dogs, which also exist.*
> *And all this weighs me down.*
> *And all this is foreign, like everything.*

Calle Mérida—make a left—ride on the sidewalk—stop

"Perhaps what is inexpressible (what I find mysterious and am not able to express) is the background against which whatever I could express has its meaning," wrote Wittgenstein somewhere. The same may be true of words that resist comprehension.

If I were to leave my apartment now, I'd ride my bike to the Librería del Tesoro. I'd chain it to a lamppost and go into the bookstore, looking for a Portuguese dictionary. It would start raining outside, as it always does on September afternoons. I'd eventually find the dictionary, look for the word, and maybe read:

Saudade: streets, cracked sidewalks, archipelagos of dog shit, the leprous walls of old buildings, the concrete sadness of a bicycle ride around the Colonia Roma at the violet hour.

I'd buy the dictionary—go outside and put it in the basket of my bike—dry the saddle a little with my sleeve—unlock the chain. I'd make my way back home. Sometimes I'd ride in the street—sometimes, on the sidewalk.

CEMENT

A man was killed on the sidewalk, near the door of our building. A single bullet in the back—at waist level. The head fell first. A sharp crack of the skull on the concrete—the sidewalk still damp from the afternoon rain. The head doesn't break as easily as the thread that ties us: it remained intact—the hair gelled back—a perfect hairdo. The teeth—visible—protruding like those of a child with a slight mental retardation. The following day his outline appeared in white chalk on the asphalt. Did the hand of the person who skirted the coastline of his body tremble? The city, its sidewalks: an enormous blackboard—instead of numbers, we add up bodies.

STUTTERING CITIES

Use alternative routes

There's a man down there, in the courtyard of the building, who's rhythmically hitting a chisel with a mallet. He's been at it for several hours. At eight in the morning, I went down to ask him what he was doing and, like someone stating the obvious, he said: Working. I didn't bother to ask the next question—the one that was really worrying me—and went back inside. I'd been standing under the shower for a few minutes before I realized that the surface of the shared courtyard we cross every day to go out into the street wouldn't be there when I next opened the door of our apartment.

I haven't yet felt like looking out into the courtyard. I wonder how we'll manage to get out of here—if perhaps the man will improvise a bridge with wooden planks or if he'll at least reach out a hand to help us across; if the cavity under the now nonexistent surface will be deep; if it'll be like that forever or if the last summer rains will end up turning our building into a blue concrete island surrounded by gray waters.

The sound of metal hitting stone doesn't stop and, as the threat of the gaping hole in this courtyard grows, in some other part of the city they are breaking up a sidewalk; in another, someone is knocking down a wall; and in the small, rounded head of a child, gently resting against the window of a metro carriage, the crack of an idea opens up—the fissure of a new word.

Bridge under repair

When I returned to live in Mexico at the age of fourteen, after twelve years away, I spoke Spanish correctly but not well. I was able to say a phrase but not twist it around, take it apart. The Spanish I spoke belonged to slow, dispassionate conversations around the family breakfast table. The Spanish spoken by people in the street was a living language, rapid and vibrant, and I found it impossible to get my teeth into it. I stuttered, I trembled when I spoke, suddenly went gravely silent in the middle of a sentence. My language was full of holes.

Men at work

If the cranium were what it seems to be—a hemispherical receptacle, a cavity, a reservoir—learning would be a way of filling an empty space. But that's not what actually happens. It's possible to imagine that every new impression digs another hole, bruises the unformed material a bit, empties us out a little more. We're born full of something—gray matter, water, blood, flesh—and in all of us, at every instant, the slow alchemy of erosion and loss is at work.

Language breaches our direct relationship with the world and words are an attempt to cross the unbridgeable gap: "Mama" cements a fragile bond with the now unattainable breast and "Me" is a mere echo of that face of mine on the other side of the mirror. In prelinguistic infancy, when the shadow of syntax hasn't yet eclipsed the radiance of the world, the rumbling of *r*s and the murmuring of *m*s are enough to say everything. A child, before it can talk, speaks the world—speaks it to himself—with a pointing finger and babbling. But one day the soft sound of the *m* becomes attached to the *a,* and is repeated—*mama.* Then, something snaps. The moment we pronounce the name of that bond, our first and most intimate one, some link with the world is broken.

Names are the glove covering a prosthesis, the wrapping of an absence. A child who learns a new word acquires a bridge to the world, but only in compensation for the chasm that opens up within him the moment that word is imprinted there. Almost all of us have heard the story about our first "Mama" (and we know that the interest of the person hearing it is usually inversely proportional to the enthusiasm of the one who relates the anecdote) but I imagine that very few of us have firsthand memories of our initial unsteady steps through language. Some people compare this initial learning experience with the ecstasy of a creative force inventing a universe. Children, they say, are like poets of Esperanto: their words exist in perfect correspondence with the world.

Hooked on the biblical myth of Paradise, we'd like to believe that the names of things are precise and imperative, that there's a word in the core of each thing and that pronouncing it is equivalent to unveiling the very essence of the object; that the act of speech is similar to the fiat of the Creator. There may be some truth in this, but the fact is that the process of acquiring a first language is as involuntary as stuttering or aphasia. Rather than a memory of Paradise, learning a language is a first banishment, an involuntary, silent exile to the interior of that nothing in the heart of everything we name. Perhaps learning to speak is realizing, little by little, that we can say nothing about anything.

Danger zone

There is a poem I like, written by Ghérasim Luca shortly before
his death. It's titled "Passionément" and begins with a stutter:

> *pas pas paspaspas pas*
> *pasppas ppas pas paspas*
> *le pas pas le faux pas le pas*
> *paspaspas le pas le mau*
> *le mauve le mauvais pas*

Luca had been in France for thirty, forty years, his whole life—it
makes no difference—when he wrote those lines. He had abandoned Romania, the Romanian language, pursued by the same
terror that expelled so many others from their countries and their
homes during the twentieth century. Luca wrote stuttering poems
full of holes. He inhabited French, a foreign language to him, and
carried it to the limits of its syntax, to the other side of grammar.
He continues:

> *je je t'aime*
> *je t'aime je t'ai je*
> *t'aime aime aime je t'aime*
> *passsionné é aime je*
> *je t'aime*
> *passionnément aimante je*
> *t'aime je t'aime passionnément*
> *je t'ai je t'aime passionné né*
> *je t'aime passionné*
> *je t'aime passionnément je t'aime*
> *je t'aime passio passsionnément*

One day he jumped into the River Seine. Leaning over the parapet of the bridge, did Ghérasim Luca's eighty-year-old body tremble before he jumped into the water? Did it stutter like the last line of his poem, which trips up on *passio* and falls: *passionnément*? The poem begins with a faux pas, a false step, and everything that follows is a fall. To where? "*When a language is so strained,*" writes the French philosopher Gilles Deleuze, "that it starts to stutter, or to murmur, or stammer . . . then *language in its entirety reaches the limit* that marks its outside and makes it confront silence." Luca's poem is the downward plunge of language toward that silence.

Mind the gap

That instant, that silence we leave in the middle of any old sentence: I was standing in . . . How do you say it? That rectangular wooden frame, sometimes the way out, but also the entrance. *Seuil* in French, *soglia* in Italian. What is the word? It was one of the first I learned—one of my earliest childhood memories is of standing under the frame of a door, while my house trembled and convulsed in rapid spasms.

It was September 19, 1985, 7:20 a.m. People were sleeping, showering, kissing their kids good-bye, seeing them off to school, tuning in radios, making coffee, making love. Then a shock—a blow—so slow—so hard—so deep—and it all came down.

We grew up knowing it could be repeated, at any time. The city could fall apart all over again. It was a temporary, transient, ephemeral place. It's hard now not to look back on Mexico City without awe—hard not to wonder how it is that the city has really not fallen, imploded, sunk, plummeted, shifted.

It hasn't. It won't. But it is full of holes and absences—like a child struggling, scuffling, stuttering to find the right word, to fill a gap.

Building materials

A few blocks from my house are the ruins of a building: a mausoleum for television sets, suitcases, telephones, books, newspapers, dolls, families. The elderly doorman of the property opposite says it was over five stories tall, a very modern building, from just before the big earthquake. Now, the pile of rubble is less than seven meters high and on top of the debris there's a Mexican flag, cats, political propaganda, a scarecrow, and a couple of dogs called Ponchadura ("Flat Tire") and Mr. President López Obrador. Hung between two metal bars, a sign announces, "We are in the process of" and the next word has been rubbed out—perhaps on purpose.

We are in the process of losing something. We go round leaving bits of dead skin on the sidewalk, dropping dead words into a conversation. Cities, like our bodies, like language, are destruction under construction. But this constant threat of earthquakes is all that's left to us. Only that kind of scene—a landscape of rubble piled on rubble—compels us to go out and look for the last remaining things. Only under that threat does it again become necessary to excavate language, to find the exact word.

Watch your step

With that strange impulse that, when we're incapable of finding the exact word, leads us back to books already read—as if we'd discover there a remedy or, perhaps, redemption—I open my French edition of *In Search of Lost Time*. This is something I first did in the library of the Pompidou Center, some years ago. I was convinced that the only way to learn French was by reading its writers. Not understanding didn't matter because the language would gradually seep through into my conscious mind, and all that was needed was a great deal of obstinacy, a notebook, and a *Petit Robert*—never a bilingual dictionary—in which to look up the words that, even after intense effort, were impossible to make out.

I understood practically nothing of the French and spent hours on a single paragraph, imagining the possible meanings of *bougie, quatour, écailles*—words I now find underlined in my copy. The écailles were, surely, to my Spanish-language ears, the escaleras, the stairs; and then "pesait comme des écailles sur mes yeux" was "weighed like stairs on my eyes," and not, as I later understood, "weighed like scales on my eyes." There are words that contain and words that overflow. Foreign words, the ones we don't know and whose meaning we can barely guess at, spill out their probable content.

I now reread some paragraphs of *À la recherche* with a certain sadness, conscious that a language that is learned will never be a stairway but always a heavy scale on the lips. I know the prepositional phrase "en train de" will never again be a train that crossed certain written or spoken utterances because at some moment it became, forever, a mere verb tense.

Dangerous junction

Legend has it that Samuel Beckett, while lying ill in the bed in which, a few days later, he would die, took up his pen to write his last poem:

comment dire –
comment dire

Later, as if he'd climbed over a wall and seen revealed, on the other side, the outside, his forever foreign language, he rewrites in English:

what is the word –
what is the word

The language that Beckett, who was his own translator, inhabits is an intermediate space between one place and another, an outside and an inside.

The threshold—that's the word.

Unloading zone

Wittgenstein used to imagine language as a great city permanently under construction. Like cities, language had modern areas, spaces in the process of renovation, historic zones. There were bridges, underground passages, walkways, skyscrapers, avenues, and narrow, silent streets.

Wittgenstein's metaphor is tempting: but things look very different from where I sit. Here, language and the city are the threshold in which I wait for the next earthquake.

I listen to the workers outside:

What now?

Now we're going to break up the whole wall—from here to here.

But where do we put the rubble?

We'll pile it up here. For now.

RELINGOS: THE CARTOGRAPHY OF EMPTY SPACES

Work suspended

On the Paseo de la Reforma, that grand avenue simulating the entrance to an imperial Mexico City that of course no longer exists, there's a quadrangle of tiny absences, small plazas, where once there were things that are now only gaps. As if the perfect, majestic smile of Madame de la Reforma now lacked a number of teeth. Only God and perhaps Salvador Novo—modernist chronicler of the city—know what was there before the appearance of those empty spaces.

These urban absences, as they might be called, were formed during the extension of the Paseo de la Reforma in the 1960s. The widening of the avenue and the addition of a new stretch were accompanied by the indiscriminate demolition of the buildings in the area. As this new road cut diagonally across the orthogonal layout of the city, some rectangular plots became triangular or trapezoidal. And, since the construction of buildings in these irregular spaces—leftovers from the Paseo—was inconceivable, the asphalt and paving-stone trapezoids and triangles remained like odd pieces of a jigsaw, the origin and purpose of which no one remembers any longer, but which, equally, no one dares to either destroy or use in any permanent way. Nowadays these residual spaces on and around certain corners of Reforma—between the enormous new junctions with the avenues Eje 1 Norte and Hidalgo—are abandoned to the perpetual comings and goings of ambulant street vendors, tourists, delivery men, petty thieves, the homeless, people taking strolls, dust, and debris.

A group of architects from the National University (UNAM), headed by Carlos González Lobo, have christened these spaces "relingos." I'm not sure where the term comes from, but I imagine it could be related to the realengas of old Castilian, a term that refers to pieces of land not belonging to the Crown, abandoned to disuse. (The strange ups and downs of words: in certain Latin American countries, *realenga* is now used to talk about an animal with no owner; in others, the word is synonymous with "layabout.")

I'm also pretty certain that *relingo* is derived from another similar concept: the terraines vagues of the Catalan architect Ignasi de Solà-Morales. Just like a relingo, the terraine vague is an ambiguous space, a piece of waste ground without defined borders or limiting fences, a species of plot on the margins of metropolitan life, even if it is physically to be found in the very center of a city, at the junction of two main avenues, or under a newly built bridge.

Coming out from Hidalgo metro station at the exit nearest to San Judas Tadeo church, there's a small triangular plaza, in the middle of which stands a tribute to the work of Mexican journalists: a statue of the nineteenth-century newspaper editor and politician Francisco Zarco surrounded by a large fountain that bubbles and spits out mouthfuls of gray water. The homeless people of the neighborhood go there with their bars of soap and towels to wash their faces and bodies beneath the bronze figure. At certain hours in the afternoon, that same plaza becomes a six-a-side football field, and at midday on Sundays it's transformed again, into the venue for a tertulia for the deaf mutes coming out from the sign language mass at San Judas.

An architect friend of mine, José Amozurrutia, once showed me the plans of a possible building he designed for that relingo. What he envisioned there was a theater that would house the hypothetical San Hipólito Deaf League, and provide a space where the congregation of the sign language mass could indefinitely prolong their Sunday gatherings, silently reading scripts and rehearsing plays. I can't think of a more brilliantly crazy idea for a relingo than a silent theater that has absolutely no possibility of ever becoming a reality.

Crane in use

Architecture, according to Roland Barthes, should be simultaneously the projection of an impossibility and the putting into practice of a functional order. In his well-known essay on the Eiffel Tower, Barthes recounts that in 1881, not long before the construction of the gigantic antenna, another French architect, Jules Bourdais, had imagined a "sun tower" for the Champ de Mars—at that time a relingo, a sort of playground or tabula rasa for speculative architects. However Bourdais may have conceived his tower, in Barthes's version—at least in the English-language translation—the structure was to have an enormous "bonfire" that would illuminate the whole city by means of a complex system of mirrors. On the top floor of the tower, crowning the great beacon decorated with wrought iron galleries, there would be a space to which Parisian invalids could ascend for air therapy.

Although Barthes's description of the sun tower lacks certain important details—for example, one wonders if the mirrors to reflect the light of the giant beacon would be installed around the city or on the tower itself, or how the invalids would get up to the top of the structure and, once there, not scorch themselves—

the idea itself is perfect in the Barthesian-architectonic sense: a semifunctional folly. Whatever the case, being incapable myself of imagining things in three dimensions, I find it fascinating to think that a person would stop in the middle of an empty space and conceive there the details of a building full of deaf mutes acting out *Macbeth* or a tower on whose pinnacle the invalids of Paris would warm their hands on a giant bonfire.

Spaces survive the passage of time in the same way a person survives his death: in the close alliance between the memory and the imagination that others forge around it. They exist as long as we keep thinking of them, imagining in them; as long as we remember them, remember ourselves there, and, above all, as long as we remember what we imagined in them. A relingo—an emptiness, an absence—is a sort of depository for possibilities, a place that can be seized by the imagination and inhabited by our phantom-follies. Cities need those vacant lots, those silent gaps where the mind can wander freely.

No soliciting

I don't think relingos are necessarily limited to exterior spaces. A few steps from the plaza where the Deaf League rehearses plays in the imagination of a certain architect is the old Miguel Cervantes Library. The building is an empty interior these days, used and reused for different purposes. Two guards stand at the front entrance: one tall and angular with a melancholy expression; the other short, with a pronounced paunch—like unwitting ghosts of Don Quixote and Sancho Panza.

When anyone enters an official-looking building in Mexico, they're greeted with variations on the questions: "On whose behalf

have you come?" "Who asked you to come here?" "Who do
you want to see?" To declare that you haven't come on anyone's
behalf, that no one recommended your visit, that you don't need
to consult any person in particular, that you're taking a walk, and
would like to go inside to take a look at the ceiling—just for the
sake of it—seems to disconcert the angels in blue who guard the
entrances to these bureaucratic paradises.

One day, after a certain amount of obstinacy on my part, the
two guards of the ex-Cervantes library finally allowed me to pass
into the ruined interior. Inside, there was not the slightest trace
of the volumes that had once resided there—perhaps just a screw
clinging to the peeling wall, against which a bookcase had rested.
But there was still an air of bookishness: a heavy atmosphere, the
stink of squandered ink, of ideas bound in hardback.

As far as I could tell, the ex-library was being used as an impro-
vised and not quite official workshop for restoring murals. Six or
seven long tables ran the length of the first floor, and on them lay
the panels of a mural from the 1930s, painted by Ramón Alva de
Canal and called *The History of Writing*.

A small, suspicious, mousy man—the "Workshop Director,"
according to the nametag pinned to his shirt—came up to chase
me away as soon as he saw me cross through the arched entrance
accompanied by one of the two guards. But the squat angel in blue,
now on my side, immediately vouched for my good intentions:
The señorita says she's come to see you, chief.

Each section of the mural recorded a different moment in the
graphological history of mankind, beginning with a simple image
of the first tremulous strokes on the wall of some cave, and ending
with a sort of strident hymn to the great industry of the modern
press. It seemed a little ironic that this very mural, *The History of*

Writing, was being restored in an ex-library completely devoid of books. The image of the empty, dilapidated library housing this mural, itself in a ruinous state, should have perhaps made up the seventh, nonexistent panel to complete the series:

1. Cave painting
2. Cuneiform writing
3. Papyri and hieroglyphs
4. The alphabet
5. Johannes Gutenberg
6. Modern printing
7. The fall of libraries and bookshops

No parking

In the middle of a sentence, after the umpteenth comma deleted and undeleted, I suddenly lose the will to continue writing. I get up from the desk, impatient and defeated, and go to the bookcase. With the persistence of a mosquito around a lightbulb, I prowl the shelves in search of that book, that page, that underlined phrase I vaguely remember, but which—if I could only reread it—would finally give me the confidence to complete my recently abandoned idea. But I find nothing and sit back down at my writing desk.

I know that the times I feel most excited about what I'm writing are when I should be most suspicious, because more often than not I'm repeating something I either said or read elsewhere, something that has been lingering in my mind for a while. I'm almost always saying something trivial just when I believe I'm on the verge of a novel idea. In contrast, the worst moment to stop writing is when I no longer feel like going on. On those occasions, it's always better to keep rapping thoughts into the keyboard, like drilling holes in the ground, until the exact word emerges. Only then, take the book off the shelf and drop into an armchair to read. In some way, I guess, writing is making space for reading.

We buy old books

Cities have often been compared to language: you can read a city, it's said, as you read a book. But the metaphor can be inverted. The journeys we make during the reading of a book trace out, in some way, the private spaces we inhabit. There are texts that will always be our dead-end streets; fragments that will be bridges; words that will be like the scaffolding that protects fragile constructions. T. S. Eliot: a plant growing in the debris of a ruined building; Salvador Novo: a tree-lined street transformed into an expressway; Tomás Segovia: a boulevard, a breath of air; Roberto Bolaño: a rooftop terrace; Isabel Allende: a (magically real) shopping mall; Gilles Deleuze: a summit; and Jacques Derrida: a pothole. Robert Walser: a chink in the wall, for looking through to the other side; Charles Baudelaire: a waiting room; Hannah Arendt: a tower, an Archimedean point; Martin Heidegger: a cul-de-sac; Walter Benjamin: a one-way street walked down against the flow.

And everything we haven't read: relingos, absences in the heart of the city.

Guaranteed repairs

Restoration: plastering over the cracks left on any surface by the erosion of time.

Writing: an inverse process of restoration. A restorer fills the holes in a surface on which a more or less finished image already exists; a writer starts from the fissures and the holes. In this sense, an architect and a writer are alike. Writing: filling in relingos.

No, writing isn't filling gaps—nor is it constructing a house, a building, just to fill up an empty space.

Perhaps Alejandro Zambra's bonsai image might come closer: "A writer is a person who rubs out. . . . Cutting, lopping: finding a form that was already there."

But words are not plants and, in any case, gardens are for the poets with orderly, landscaped hearts. Prose is for those with a builder's spirit.

Writing: drilling walls, breaking windows, blowing up buildings. Deep excavations to find—to find what? To find nothing.

A writer is a person who distributes silences and empty spaces.

Writing: making relingos.

RETURN TICKET

Raw materials

I've spent weeks putting off the inevitable ordering of my bookshelves. I sit on the only chair in the apartment, my feet resting
on a box labeled "Kitchem things" and stare at the empty shelves.

Leases

I know people who have made an art of the extremely tedious
task of viewing apartments; people who pass through a city visit-
ing houses or rooms to let, unfurnished and rather dingy, only to
go back to their own accommodation—perfectly habitable, and
surely prettier—and imagine where they would put the piano,
the writing desk, the bookcase in that other empty place. "Things,
things, things," complained the poet Robert Creeley, "and nowhere
to go."

Empty places have a fascination that at once stimulates and dis-
concerts us. The gaze—which is nothing more than an extension, a
hand, of the mind—takes pleasure in and entertains itself filling up
hollow spaces. Maybe this intolerance of absence is merely a mal-
formation of the human mind. Pretentious Heideggerians might
say it's just an ontic expression of a more deep-seated ontological
condition, impossible to change: horror vacui expressed as the
ocular amusement and mental pastime of filling spaces. Whatever
the truth, I can't claim to be free of guilt. Although I hate moves,

and empty apartments depress me, I've also found solace in furnishing certain spaces in my imagination.

Change of address

My face is different since I moved into this apartment. Something happened to it during the move. As if I'd lost the contour of my forehead amid the boxes; as if with so much dust, the curve of my chin had blurred. I study myself in the bathroom mirror while I brush my teeth and try to connect my nose to my brow, the right eye to the irremediable shadow beneath it, always darker than on the left: I have a face full of gaps.

A coffee, a newspaper on the table: I browse yesterday's news—skip the politics—go to the culture pages. Between a succinct article on Lichtenberg's aphorisms and an interview with Umberto Eco, I find the last portrait taken of Marguerite Duras. Today I look like that final portrait: a crumpled piece of paper.

I cut out the photo with the kitchen scissors and put it between the pages of a notebook; maybe it will come in useful some time, though I'll most likely forget about it. The problem for people like me who collect scraps of paper with no method or ultimate objective is that our boxes and notebooks come to look ever more like us: a disorganized collage and never a coherent catalog of marvels. If I find the photo of Duras again some day while rummaging in a notebook or a box, it will be by pure chance. And I don't know what that gaze, that hand holding a fountain pen as if it were her last grip on the world, would say to me.

Open all hours

I look for Marguerite Duras's *Écrire* in the boxes of books; I know it's going to be difficult to find, but yet again I'm not going to organize my bookshelves. What I need—and haven't found—is a system: Does Borges go after Arlt, Poe, Stevenson, or the *Thousand and One Nights*? Do Shakespeare and Dante belong on the same shelf? It's difficult to know how much influence the title of a book has on the one next to it. Maybe books prefer disorder to the "mild boredom of order" that Walter Benjamin described while unpacking his library. In any case, accidental order can produce the best finds. There's a well-known anecdote: metaphysics was the accidental invention of a librarian who, on receiving Aristotle's masterwork, didn't know where to shelve it. Having deliberated for some time, he placed the newly arrived volumes after the philosopher's *Physics*. To remind himself where they were, he noted in his catalog: "tá méta tá física" (literally: "that which comes after physics"). By that same logic, which books would comprise the meta-Shakespearean category?

Maybe organizing the bookshelves is more effort than it's worth. True, books look attractive on the shelves and make a space feel inhabited, but when they wake from their vertical slumber, they have lives of their own. Some books even give life to others—like the ones Silvina Ocampo writes about, which, when left to their own devices, begin to fornicate and reproduce.

That book on the bed is a generous and undemanding lover; that other one, on the bedside table, an infallible oracle I consult from time to time, or a talisman against midnight crises; the one on the couch, a pillow for long, dreamless naps. Some books get forgotten for months. They're left in the bathroom or on top of the fridge in the kitchen for a while and are replaced by others when our indifference eventually wears them away. The few we really do read are places we always return to.

Storage space

Between pages forty-two and forty-three of my edition of Daniel Pennac's *Comme un Roman,* a strip of Pepto-Bismol tablets past their expiration date; in John Dos Passos's *Manhattan Transfer,* a terse postcard from New Delhi; on the last page of *Luces de Bohemia* by Ramón del Valle-Inclán, an address and telephone number; in Julio Cortázar's *Rayuela,* chapter sixty-eight has been torn out.

Rereading begins in the comments written in the margins, the underlined phrases and scribbled footnotes; but especially in the objects left behind between the pages.

Real estate

After rooting about in one of the boxes, I finally find *Écrire* in a pile, between Natalia Ginzburg's *Lessico famigliare* and Robert Walser's *The Walk.* It's been many years since I read Marguerite Duras. I'm afraid to reread her in case, this time, she bores me or seems affected. Or worse, in case I remember the person I was when I first read her, and dislike myself in her.

I open the book but don't read anything. Instead, I find between the pages an Indian railway ticket from my teenage years:

> Return Ticket. Train No. 6346. Trivandrum Central to Victoria Central Station. One six zero Rupees only, no refunds please. Happy Journey.

Going back to a book is like returning to the cities we believe to be our own, but which, in reality, we've forgotten and been forgotten by. In a city—in a book—we vainly revisit passages, looking for nostalgias that no longer belong to us. Impossible to return to a place and find it as you left it—impossible to discover in a book exactly what you first read between its lines. We find, at best, fragments of objects among the debris, incomprehensible marginal notes that we have to decipher to make our own again.

Furnished apartments

"One does not find solitude, one makes it," writes Duras. Flipping through the pages of *Écrire,* that's the first phrase I find underlined. I can still catch an echo of its original intensity, but I'd be lying if I said I knew why it was that phrase, and not some other, that struck me so forcefully at the start of the long train journey back to Mumbai. I probably understood something for the first time, but have now forgotten what. I probably found words for something that I'd long been trying to articulate and that ceased to matter once I'd found those words.

My memories of the two years I lived in India as a teenager are fragmentary, ephemeral, almost trivial. I conserve impossible images. There are faces that I only manage to recall in two dimensions. I visualize myself in the third person, always in the same clothes—a long, scrambled egg–yellow dress, my hair tied back with a white handkerchief—walking along the same street, which, I suspect, is a superimposition of many streets. I know that some memories are a later fabrication: fantasies embroidered during a casual conversation, exaggerations sculpted in the different versions of a paragraph I wrote over and again in my letters home.

I do, however, remember the books I read during the years I lived there and the voracity and devotion with which I underlined certain sections of them—sometimes entire paragraphs were underscored twice, once in pencil and once in ink. I think it was Gertrude Stein who used to say that people become civilized before they turn twenty. I don't know if I'd become civilized by then—or if I ever shall—but I did become a reader during those years and have never again read a book with the same sense of rapture. My world was shaped by books—not vice versa. A train journey—the chai vendors; the blue plastic seats that made your legs sweat; the impossibly large families picnicking on the floor of the carriages; the immense, beautiful, complex, fucked-up country out there— was a mirror to Duras's *Écrire,* Joyce's *Portrait of the Artist,* Orwell's essays, Borges's *Ficciones.* I used to sit on the steps of one of the open doors at the end of a carriage and light a cigarette, take out a pen and pencil for underlining, and read until my eyes burned.

Remembering, according to etymologists, is "bringing back to the heart." The heart, however, is merely an absentminded organ that pumps blood. But rereading is not like remembering. It's more like rewriting ourselves: the subtle alchemy of reinventing our past through the twice-underscored words written by others.

Flits and moves

The portrait of Duras between the pages of a notebook. The notebook on top of a box full of books, which serves as a table. And on top of the notebook, a half-empty coffee cup. I take out the portrait and study it once more. Today I look like Duras.

I go back to my own face: I see there the many faces that have formed me, the family tree of features, the genealogy of every facial expression and gesture. There's a line drawn by my mother's cheerfulness, shadows beneath my eyes as heavy as my father's weariness, a pair of attentive lines on my brow that the two of them impressed on me. There's a curve of the mouth, which some grandmother has slipped in; a look in my eyes that recalls the exiled loneliness of my grandfather; an expression that is the early-onset dementia of my aunt. But this face, my face, like all faces, is not only a collection of traces—it's also the first draft of a future face. The mutable substance of the skin is always unfinished—its folds reveal a direction: an uncertain but already present future. Like the raw material of a sculptor, which, from the first moment, suggests the figure that will emerge after being worked, a face encloses its future faces. In my young face I instinctively read a first wrinkle of doubt, a first smile of indifference: lines of a story I'll rewrite and understand on a future rereading.

OTHER ROOMS

There now is your insular city of the Manhattoes . . .

Herman Melville

Zero

W. G. Sebald says that the emigrant is that person who seeks out his own kind—wherever he goes. I seek out doormen, who are usually emigrants of some kind, metaphorically if not literally. The doormen of the buildings in this neighborhood—especially those on the night shift, the strangest of all—make me feel an urge for human contact I'm unable to restrain. In my permanent capacity as an alien nonresident in New York, I find solace in these men and women who guard the transition from night to day, the threshold between the street and the interiors.

The night-shift doorman of my building belongs to that endangered species of people who still smoke tobacco. In the ten-minute periods of beatific temporal suspension that make up the last cigarette of my working day and the first of his shift—the eternal return of his dark night of the soul—I've managed to strike up a friendship with him. What you have to do, he says when I get back, late and defeated, and we're smoking a cigarette together—shivering on the steps of the building—is to get out of here as often as you can. That way you get to know yourself better. Only come back to have a bath and eat, never to sleep, because the more often you spend the night in different places—rooms, hostels, hotels, borrowed couches, other people's beds—the better.

Sometimes the doorman and I light a second cigarette.

We'd learn to reach deeper into ourselves, he continues, by looking at our reflections now and again in the mirror of someone else's bathroom, washing our hair with their shampoo, or laying our head—some nights—on another person's pillow. We should all participate in a certain amount of housing polygamy if we want to be true to the millenarian edict: Know thyself.

How do you mean?

Didn't you study philosophy? he asks me.

More or less, I answer.

One

The residential buildings in this neighborhood are pseudo-modernized piles dating from the beginning of the twentieth century, with fake wood or iron cornices imitating stone, heavy, slow-moving glass doors, brick facades redundantly painted brick-color: the first triumph of property speculation and the last whimper of the age of ornamental architecture. The apartments are fitted with fluorescent lighting to cut costs and create a favorable environment for the residents' varying states of depression. In the ready-furnished interiors like mine, there isn't much. The official inventory lists: folding dining table, folding chair, four-shelf bookcase, armchair upholstered in green, single bed, fridge, stove.

Two

The windows don't appear on the inventory. They don't count. None of them are wide or transparent enough to fulfil the purpose of a window: allowing space to come in. What's the use of living on the seventh floor if you have to lean out and crane your neck to be able to see—there in the distance—the horizon, or—way above—the sky. (Not once have I seen a bird, though, mysteriously, I once saw a fly, its tiny legs glued to the other side of the windowpane.)

During the daytime, other people's walls and windows—their possible solitudes—dominate the view that the glass rectangles offer. Neither do the windows behave like windows when it gets dark. At night, when I switch on the lights in the living room, the windows reflect the interior of my own apartment instead of revealing the exterior. There's no way out, just mirrors: the windows force you to see yourself reflected in them every time you leave the desk to go to the bathroom or make another coffee. This would be fortunate, if only these words by either Walter Benjamin or Friedrich Nietzsche—I never know which—were true: "To be happy is to become aware of oneself without fright." But no one ever achieves that. I see myself cross from the living room to the kitchen—from the kitchen to the living room—my skinny body, languid, lacking aplomb, intermittently reflected in each window.

The fact that you see yourself mirrored in the windows at night and almost never see the outside world is most probably an architectural strategy for creating an illusion of privacy in a city where the view is a constant invitation to peek into other lives. And this has to do with the balance between the dose of happiness and unhappiness a person can be granted. Leaning out, peering into other windows is an invitation to speculate about other people's possessions, their better lives, happier existences—and it's a fact that the happiness of others is, by a simple act of comparison, the main reason for our personal unhappiness.

Despite the praiseworthy achievements of architectural reformers, it's easy to cheat privacy in these buildings. If my neighbors have their lights on and I don't, they can only make out their own reflection and don't see me watching them, so as soon as I turn out the lights in my apartment, the mute spectacle of my neighbors' lives switches on. Lately, I've been spending a few hours each night spying on them. Yet, for all my laudable hacking of their privacy, I've been sad to discover that my neighbors' lives are as unexciting as mine. Like me, like everyone else in the city, they all possess personal computers, so nothing ever happens in the windows opposite.

It's clear that the personal computer is the great modern attack on good old-fashioned voyeurism. From the moment these machines were installed in our homes, the irreversible process of the degeneration of character began and ruled out the possibility of anyone doing anything interesting for the delight of their voyeuristic neighbor. Impossible, since the advent of Facebook and Twitter, for anyone to commit a spectacular crime in his living room or to conduct a good affair (dirty, delectable, and detectable). Indiscreet rear windows to other lives no longer exist because everything happens inside those smaller, more circumspect Windows on our computer screens.

Three

On the streets of this part of the city—a pluperfect grid—everyone is in rectilinear transit and no one converges on a single point. There's almost nowhere suitable for an out-of-hours get-together or meeting—except, maybe, the laundry rooms in the basements of buildings, where the washing machines are located. But these Dantesque infernos of cyclical hygienic tortures are almost always empty, and even when I come across a neighbor there, I go out of my way to avoid conversation since the topic will inevitably dry up more quickly than the laundry and I'll be forced to start saying things I really don't want to.

There's nothing to talk about with the people who live in this building. Gilberto Owen, the Mexican poet who resided in this very same area over eighty years ago, knew why: the worst defect of neighbors here is their incapacity for properly bad-mouthing each other. Not only is that fundamentally true—but the current reality is worse still. Today our neighbors are always happy, always excited about something, always doing great, really great, never openly disillusioned, never ever unsuccessful, properly depressed, or decently full of spite.

So, I've found that if I want to live in harmony with the world, the best thing is to scarcely cross glances with the Neo-Manhattoes of this neighborhood, not to exchange a single word, still less a telephone number or e-mail address in the supermarket aisle. If I'm forced to share an elevator, I give, at most, a cordial nod. If I go to the laundry room, I stick to the silent ceremony of the soap powder. And outside in the street, nothing beats carrying an umbrella, under whose sheltering arch I can hide from the gazes of others.

Four

It's often said that modernity began with the erosion of the frontiers between the private and the public and the consequent leap into the abyss of ubiquitous intimacy. Could be. But nowadays, to be true to the Delphic exhortation my night doorman regularly evokes—Know thyself—it's no longer appropriate to retreat into the interior. Even in our private spaces, we're increasingly engulfed by the expansionist empire of Google and spied on by the phantasmagorical armies of all our close and distant acquaintances. There's nowhere to go—and the windows give no shelter, the screens no relief.

Five

Ishmael, the sailor, knew that he should set out to sea when he began to feel the irresistible urge to systematically remove the hats of passersby with the tip of his umbrella. I know I should leave my house when *Moby-Dick* takes on a more robust existence than my own: "[et] le monde bat de l'autre côté de ma porte"—"and the world beats on the other side of my door."

Sometimes I go out into the street just for the sake of it.

But even there you can't be with yourself. In spite of Edgar Allan Poe's early and wise dictum—we are always alone when we are a man in a crowd—every time I go out on my own, I have to discover all over again that being alone is not equivalent to being with myself. Or worse, that my own company is not necessarily the best company.

We live in a world in which there has been a complete inversion of the status of the street as the public space and the house as the ultimate private space. In this redistribution of the private–public categories it's difficult to know when we're really inside and when out. I say this without the least hint of nostalgia. In the street we can no longer commune with solitude, and even in our own homes, we can't be with ourselves without the windows of computers claiming our already deficient attention or the neighbors installing themselves in the backyard of our brains: there's the Chinese guy opposite opening his fridge, and there he goes to sit in front of his rectangular, electronic furnace. So our only option is to construct small, fleeting intimacies in other spaces. My doorman is right.

Six

A doorman is the owner of the only privileged space in this city. Standing proud and upright, smoking in front of the facade of his building or leaning back in a chair in the lobby, the doorman is the guardian, the modern Cerberus, who watches over the imprecise limits between the public world and the private.

If there still exists a gaze blessed with liminal wisdom, it is the gaze of night-shift doormen. They are the only true freethinkers— generous men capable of conversing intelligently at midnight; empathetic accomplices, offering the consolation of a companion- ship replete with the same reprehensible vices you yourself have and defend. In contrast to all the other people in my building, the night-shift doorman smokes, doesn't have a computer, com- plains about all sorts of things, and bad-mouths the neighbors to anybody willing to listen. The latter being worth its weight in gold: we never learn more about ourselves than when listening to one person bad-mouthing another.

Only in that liminal space, under the umbrella of his company, do I feel safe from the claustrophobic categories of outside and inside. And although I still don't fully understand why my doorman, who doesn't even sleep at night, urges me to borrow bedrooms and rent hotel rooms far from my home, I suspect that he's absolutely right.

I've often thought about taking his advice: You've got to build a life in other rooms, I repeat to myself. You have to look at yourself in the mirrors of other bathrooms more often, he reminds me. And when the two of us have stubbed out our cigarettes and gone inside, he poses like a sphinx at the reception desk and I, who should, at that very moment, take the subway to any other place and sleep in any other room, call the elevator and press seven.

PERMANENT RESIDENCE

*The first time I fell madly in love with Venice; now
I believe I am always in love with her, but were I to marry her,
it would be a marriage of convenience.*

Rubén Darío

Ezra Pound (1885–1972)

"I am resolved not to die," wrote Miguel de Unamuno. Although there are people who find some form of salvation in the last and happy turn of the screw—the postscript to an existence that has borne rich fruit—the rest of us should take care that the little we leave behind doesn't turn against us. If not, we'll go on uttering metaphysical vagaries two meters underground, like Unamuno: "I neither want to die nor do I want to want to die; I want to live for ever and ever and ever."

None of this would worry me if it were not that some days ago, while I was wandering aimlessly around the center of Mexico City, passing the time before a doctor's appointment, I ended up going into what I thought was a garden and turned out to be a small cemetery. Not just any cemetery, but San Fernando, the very graveyard that houses the tombs of Mexico's national heroes and founding fathers: Juárez, Miramón, Comonfort, Guerrero, and Zaragoza. I had a book with me and all I wanted was to sit and read in a silent space until the hour of my appointment arrived. The guard at the entrance, like all those who stand vigil at the doors of official precincts in this city, barred my way and interrogated me. I'm not looking for anything or anyone in particular, I told him, I just want to sit here and read. He replied that the San Fernando wasn't a library, but that if I wanted to go in to see the tomb of the Father of the Americas—Benito Juárez—I should put my name, the date, time of entry, and signature in the small book he held out to me. And while you're at it, he said, put the exit time here.

I went into the cemetery in the spirit of an impromptu outing (Oscar Wilde on my side, like in that Smiths song). After strolling around the tombs of the men who forged the perpetually crumbling Mexican nation, I found a quiet corner and opened my book. It was perhaps in a moment of distraction from my reading that I raised my head and saw the inscription on the gravestone in front of me: Joaquín Ramírez (1834–1866). "The late-lamented, distinguished, but overlooked artist left this world to go to his true country." I can't think of a more simultaneously elegant but cruel way to predict someone's entry into hell. Terrified, I imagined what might become of me at thirty-two, the age when poor Ramírez—whoever he was—had shuffled off this mortal coil, and what my relatives could write about me on my grave if I were to die within ten years.

At that time, I'd just returned from a long trip to Italy, where I'd been researching an improbable future book on the periods Joseph Brodsky spent in Venice. I'd visited the poet's grave in San Michele cemetery, the hotels where he'd stayed, the cafés he'd frequented; I'd interviewed his Venetian acquaintances, doormen, waiters, stall holders, and had even found a grand-niece of Boris Pasternak, who initially promised to show me the letters that had passed between the two Russians but, in the end, could—or would—only offer me coffee and good conversation. When the trip was over and I reread my notes, I swore I'd never write anything about Venice, simply because there's nothing more vulgar and futile than encouraging the production of even one more page about the city, perhaps the most frequently cited place in the world of books. Writing about Venice is like emptying a glass of water into the sea.

However, that day, in the San Fernando cemetery, sitting before the grave of Joaquín Ramírez, I thought I heard the voice of my conscience, as if from beyond the tomb, condemning me to the fate of all the late-lamented if I didn't leave my last wishes in writing. So, I shall dare to write these final Venetian paragraphs.

Carlo Nordio (1904–1929)

I arrived on the island in the least poetic and most economical manner: under a blazing midday sun, slightly ill, and by bus. I crossed the bridge from the Piazzale Roma car park to the district with cheap pensions: not a single vacant room. I was beginning to feel a sharp pain in my lower abdomen. On the recommendation of a very kind Venetian receptionist—a rare combination—I ended up knocking on the door of the Convento delle Suore Canossiane. I paid a lot of euros for a room like a cell, left my suitcases under a gigantic crucifix, washed my face, and went out to give the pain the slip.

Getting lost in Venice is a cliché from which I should have been saved by my good sense of direction. But something must have gone wrong. When I finally found my way back to the convent, the clocks were striking midnight and the great wooden portal protecting the nuns from the secular outer world was already locked. There was no bell to press or ring so that I could demand of the Canossian sisters my right to a reserved, dearly bought room.

I took this defeat in good spirits. I thought I could spend the night reading Brodsky on a bench until I fell asleep—or died. Whatever malady I had, it was undoubtedly terminal, and I was

destined to die on that island. What's more, it all fit: the book I had
with me was the Italian version of Brodsky's *Watermark,* entitled
Fondamenta degli Incurabili (*Street of the Incurables*). My time had
come and I ought to devote those last moments to taking stock
of my life and not continue to put off thinking about things that
really mattered. It would be a kind of sudden, triumphal death in
Venice.

Achille Beccari (1860–1893)

When people gifted with at least a little intelligence repeatedly
think about the problems of identity, life, or death, sooner or later
they're likely to arrive at reasonable, even original conclusions.
I've never been able to spend very much time mulling over such
topics: I get distracted after a couple minutes, odd places in my
body start to itch. And so I've never arrived at any truly interesting
conclusion about myself.

Although it might seem paradoxical, growing up in a family
of liberal-minded atheists, committed but never militant, tends
to have devastating consequences. Being raised without a rigid
backdrop of religious, political, or spiritual beliefs makes it hard
to have a real crisis later in life. There is no way forward if your
point of departure is the comfortable passivity of someone who
has been a self-professed agnostic since the age of twelve, without
ever having considered those important—one might say grave—
matters, such as God, death, love, failure, or fear. For a precocious
agnostic, the virtues offered by skepticism become terrifying
hands that strangle and suffocate the already rare capacity of
an individual to question things. Conversely, intelligent people
who grow up thinking one thing and, on reaching a certain age,

realize that everything they believed is open to doubt—stark, brutal doubt—can truly enjoy a profound crisis that, in the worst cases, leads them to know themselves a little better. As T. S. Eliot contends, the spirit of belief is impossible to separate from the demon of doubt.

Sergei Diaghilev (1872–1929)

Unfortunately for me, I never had any major crises. And I had even fewer qualms about assuming a national identity. Although we almost never had a fixed residence anywhere and, thanks to a nonno from Lombardy, my family and I have Italian nationality, I always knew that Mexico was my country. This was not through some authentic act of faith, but rather a sort of spiritual laziness. In contrast to many of my contemporaries, in my childhood I was even dressed up in the traditional Mexican china poblana costume for the Independence Day celebrations on September 15 and I put up no resistance nor displayed the least sign of rebellion (if I had a child like that, without a trace of rebellious spirit, I'd be worried). From my infancy, I accepted the whole ethno-cultural package of Mexicanness, as others accept baby food.

My only crisis lasted fifteen or twenty minutes one summer afternoon on the Periférico, Mexico City's—formerly orbital—expressway. At the Altavista exit, there's a small, scrubby garden in the shape of a lozenge—a piece of land that may have been left over or was perhaps simply missing when they finished mapping out the junction of the access road with the avenue leading to the San Ángel flower market. A few years earlier, for some reason I'm not aware of, my father had managed to persuade someone to donate three palm trees and a bit of grass to beautify this neglected, leftover corner, this relingo. When the restoration of the garden had been completed, my father declared—in a private act of paternal love that, had it been public, would have been a very Mexican gesture of tremendously cringeworthy nepotism—that each of the trees was to be named after one of his three daughters. Time passed and one Sunday he finally convinced us to go with him to visit the spot. When we arrived, he lined us up on the sidewalk of the access road and said: Look, girls, give me your hands (when he gets emotional, my father asks us to give him our hands). Here are the three of you—Daniela, Mariana, Valeria— heroic palm trees growing, undaunted, in this asphalt desert, this shadowy underworld of the elevated section of the Periférico.

But there weren't three. The smallest palm wasn't there. Perhaps they'd been lying to me all along and, in fact, there had only been enough money for two—though my father still swears there were three: he says he has a precise memory of it and wouldn't lie about something like that. Granted. If, then, it wasn't a lie, and I assigned some kind of symbolic value to the fact that my palm was no longer there, I knew I should be worried about my future. If my palm tree hadn't taken root, I would never put down roots in Mexico City—that vast asphalt relingo left over or simply missing from the country.

Enea Lombardi (1902–1943)

During the years between that trivial crisis and my first night in Venice, I believed in the kitsch notion that literature could be like a great house, a territory without frontiers that offers shelter to those of us who don't know how to inhabit any particular place— those of us who prefer to live "Anywhere out of the World," as

Baudelaire called that poem in which he writes that "This life is a hospital where every patient is possessed with the desire to change beds." It's a mystery to me what inner mechanisms make us capable of convincing ourselves that certain metaphors—which some people use lightly, just to illustrate their point or decorate their poems—are applicable to our own lives. Nothing was further from the truth, in my life at least, than the metaphor of literature as a habitable place or permanent dwelling. At best, the books I read were much like certain hotel rooms into which we enter, exhausted, at midnight and from which we are expelled at midday—or vice versa, as had happened to me on this occasion in Venice.

The thought of dying on a bench reading Brodsky was romantic. But books don't give us a mattress to sleep on, a shower with hot water, or relief from real pain. After thinking things over a little, I decided to phone the only person I knew on the island.

Roberta Mazzini (1842–1899)

Amerigo and I hadn't seen each other for many years. But you're welcome to stay with me, he said, just walk toward the fish's tail, ask for Calle Vecchia, and you'll be here before you know it. Have you got a map? Yes, I said, and as soon as I'd hung up I began to sleepwalk my way between the suffocating walls of the city, with no idea of where I was going. For a while, I simply followed an elderly English couple, my personal Virgils, who were complaining bitterly because someone had drawn graffiti on one of those walls.

I got lost—again. I had to call Amerigo—again—from another public telephone. If you don't come and fetch me this instant,

I said, I'm going to die—I'm outside the Hotel Escandinavia. I must have sounded very bad, because in a few minutes—Arrivo subito—Amerigo appeared from an alley.

As we began walking toward his house, I asked him about the possibility of seeing a doctor immediately. You're still a hypochondriac, Luiselli, you don't look all that ill. He explained that private physicians in Venice were for wealthy tourists and cost a fortune, so the next day we'd put my Italian passport to good use and register me as a resident of the Commune of Venice. Then, we'd organize a medical card and—finally—I could visit Dottor Stefano, his general practitioner on the southeast tip of the island (the fish's tail). I tried to explain that those things took months, and insisted the pain was unbearable and I was at death's door. But he replied with a "Never lose hope, Luiselli," and said this in such a thoroughly Venetian, operatic tone, that I was forced into silence.

The next day I went to the civil registry office with Amerigo. There was no queue and in ten minutes I was given a tax code. Then, we visited an office where we were declared to be living in legal cohabitation—coppia di fatto, they say—so that I could be assigned a postal address. There was no one in that office either, except for three female bureaucrats reading the newspaper. The one who attended us congratulated us on our newly acquired status as a couple and, after stamping two or three forms, said to me: Adesso, sei veneziana. I was still digesting the fact that the kind signora had just told me I was now a Venetian when we arrived at the Ministry of Health, where it took two minutes to get me a medical card. So, in a matter of a couple of hours, I became a part of the Italian tax system, got myself a husband, an address in Venice, and a doctor. And not only that, but I was able to witness an invisible city, probably in danger of extinction: the empty, damp, silent Venice of government offices. If there's still a Venice worth seeing, it's in those bureaucratic paradises. Sometime in the late afternoon, I sank into the arms of Dottor Stefano, who cured me with a little yellow pill.

Valeria Luiselli (1983–)

There are writers who invent cities and take possession of entire eras, wielding their pens with the sword-edge of genius: the London of Johnson and Chesterton, the Paris of Rousseau or Baudelaire, Joyce's Dublin. There are others who, by force of reading, solitude, and tranquil hours, conquer literary territories, philosophical paradigms, impossible spaces: Montaigne's tower, Sor Juana Inés de la Cruz's cell, Chateaubriand's tomb. Others construct stories like extraordinary palaces or desert islands that they then inhabit, like one more character in the warp and weft of their own plot—perhaps Sebald, Bolaño, Pitol, and Vila-Matas are of that ilk. There are a few who, with the patience of a gardener, cultivate the art of the aphorism throughout a whole life and watch it bloom—late, perhaps, but fully—beneath their feet: such is the case of Wittgenstein and an Italo-Argentinian whose name I can never remember. And there are yet others who, dedicated to the arduous task of clearing the weeds from their own language, end up putting down roots in apparently desert plains, which are, in fact, rich in poetic humus: the sun-beaten piles of broken images T. S. Eliot describes in his London Wasteland.

I, who have rather fruitlessly attempted some of those things, now have the joy of being an official resident of one of the most literary of cities, though neither through the blessing of a graceful pen nor the fidelity of the muses. And, worse still, not even through the sweat of my brow and fist, but because of a terrible—although very frequent, hence, unglamorous—ailment of the bladder: the ignoble bacterial cystitis. But in fact, it comforts me to think that if I die before my time, at least I'll have taken up false permanent residence in the Most Serene Republic of Venice, and will thus be able to fulfil my wish to be buried in some relingo, perhaps not far from Joseph Brodsky, in the commoners' section of the cemetery of San Michele.

ABOUT THE TRANSLATOR

CHRISTINA MACSWEENEY has an MA in literary translation from the University of East Anglia and specializes in Latin American fiction. Her translations have previously appeared in a variety of online sites and literary magazines. She has also translated Valeria Luiselli's novel, *Faces in the Crowd*.

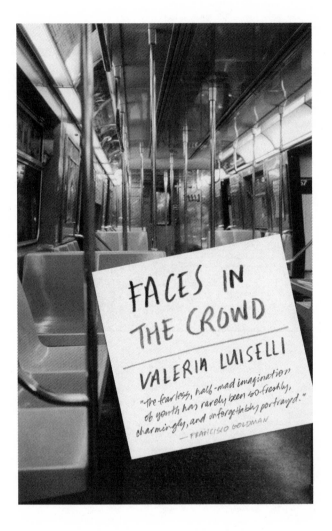

FACES IN
THE CROWD

VALERIA LUISELLI

"The fearless, half-mad imagination
of youth has rarely been so freshly,
charmingly, and unforgettably portrayed."
—FRANCISCO GOLDMAN

FACES IN THE CROWD

A novel by Valeria Luiselli

Paper • 978-1-56689-354-1   eBook • 978-1-56689-355-8

A YOUNG MOTHER in contemporary Mexico City recalls her days as a translator in New York, while in a recent past, a young translator wanders Harlem seeking out traces of the poet Gilberto Owen. And in 1950s Philadelphia, Owen dreams of New York, and the young woman in a red coat he sees in the windows of passing trains.

As the voices of the narrators overlap and merge, they drift into a single stream, a mingling that is also a disappearing act, and an elegiac evocation of love and loss. Valeria Luiselli's debut signals the arrival of a major international writer and an unexpected and necessary voice in contemporary fiction.

"A multiangled portrait of the artist as a young woman, as a con artist, as a young mother and wife, this book immerses the reader in the most enchanting and persuasive intimacy. The fearless, half-mad imagination of youth has rarely been so freshly, charmingly, and unforgettably portrayed. Valeria Luiselli is a precociously masterful and entirely original new writer."
—FRANCISCO GOLDMAN, author of *Say Her Name*

"A masterwork of fractured identities and shifting realities, *Faces in the Crowd* is a lyric meditation on love, mortality, ghosts, and the desire to transform our human wreckage into art, to be saved by creation. Valeria Luiselli is a stunning and singular voice. Her work burns with an urgency that demands our attention. Read her. Right now."
—LAURA VAN DEN BERG, author of *The Isle of Youth*

Coffee House Press

THE MISSION of Coffee House Press is to publish exciting, vital, and enduring authors of our time; to delight and inspire readers; to contribute to the cultural life of our community; and to enrich our literary heritage. By building on the best traditions of publishing and the book arts, we produce books that celebrate imagination, innovation in the craft of writing, and the many authentic voices of the American experience.

Visit us at coffeehousepress.org.

Funders

Coffee House Press is an independent, nonprofit literary publisher. Our books are made possible through the generous support of grants and gifts from many foundations, corporate giving programs, state and federal support, and through donations from individuals who believe in the transformational power of literature. Coffee House Press receives major operating support from Amazon, the Bush Foundation, the National Endowment for the Arts, the Jerome Foundation, the McKnight Foundation, from Target, and in part from a grant provided by the Minnesota State Arts Board through an appropriation by the Minnesota State Legislature from the State's general fund and its arts and cultural heritage fund with money from the vote of the people of Minnesota on November 4, 2008, and a grant from the Wells Fargo Foundation of Minnesota. Support for this title was received from the National Endowment for the Arts, a federal agency. Coffee House also receives support from: several anonymous donors; Elmer L. and Eleanor J. Andersen Foundation; Mary & David Anderson Family Foundation; Around Town Agency; the E. Thomas Binger and Rebecca Rand Fund of the Minneapolis Foundation; the Patrick and Aimee Butler Family Foundation; the Buuck Family Foundation, Dorsey & Whitney, LLP; Fredrikson & Byron, P.A.; the Kenneth Koch Literary Estate; the Lenfestey Family Foundation; the Nash Foundation; the Rehael Fund of the Minneapolis Foundation; Schwegman, Lundberg & Woessner, P.A.; the Archie D. & Bertha H. Walker Foundation; the Woessner Freeman Family Foundation; and many generous individual donors.

To you and our many readers across the country,
we send our thanks for your continuing support.

Coffee House Press Publishers Circle

LITERATURE
is not the same thing as
PUBLISHING